ALSO BY JERRY GILLIES

MONEYLOVE: How to Get the Money You Deserve for Whatever You Want

MEN ON WOMEN: 101 Men Reveal Their Deepest Desires, Feelings, and Fears

PSYCHOLOGICAL IMMORTALITY: Using Your Mind to Extend Your Life

TRANSCENDENTAL SEX: A Meditative Approach to Increasing Sensual Pleasure

FRIENDS: The Power and Potential of the Company You Keep

MY NEEDS, YOUR NEEDS, OUR NEEDS: A Handbook For Discovering Each Other and Enhancing Your Love Potential

MONEYLOVE 3.0

New Digital Age Sequel From A Pioneering Prosperity Teacher

Editor's Note:

Moneylove 3.0 was originally published in digital format. It is so jammed-packed with vital information and contains such a large amount of incredible content that each of the 12 Chapters could easily be books on their own. A print edition of this work would come in at over 700 pages - too cumbersome for many reasons! As a result we have elected to break it up into 3 Volumes that will each include the Introduction and several Chapters.

Welcome to Volume 1, which will cover Chapters 1-5, the Instruction Manual for the Book, the Introduction and the Additional Resources Section of the Original work.

This is a book unlike any you've read before and we strongly encourage you to follow Jerry's instructions on how to use the book and to heed his call to "Do the Damn Exercises!". It is our great hope that the ideas and exercises contained in this book can fill you with "Robust Expectations" and lead you to the "Joyful and Triumphant" results the author intended.

This book is dedicated to six good friends and mentors who would definitely have been a part of it if they were still around. Wait, they are still around in spirit and actually are a part of it.

Ray Bradbury
Leo Buscaglia
Norman Cousins
Ken Keyes, Jr.
Og Mandino
Ric Masten

Hip Hip Hooray! My Acknowledgments

I know it's usual for an author to state he or she couldn't have written their book without the support and assistance of a sometimes long list of people. Not true in my case! I definitely could have written this without any help at all. Of course, it would have then been a very short and not nearly as good a book--but it could've been done.

One of the things I am most proud of in my life, and a way in which I have definitely left a major thumbprint on the world, is my excellent taste in choosing teachers and mentors and friends and colleagues. I have been so blessed with so many supporters and fantastic contributors to this work.

Yes, Moneylove 3.0 might have still been written without the support of Rupa Cousins, Barry Dunlop, Christina Makrides, Leo Quinn, and Mary Ann Somervill--but not nearly as well or nearly as soon.

My list of contributors, whom I also call faculty members, and whose wisdom added vast value and profound dimensions to this volume, I will list alphabetically:

Martin Boroson, Tony Busse, Marianne Cantwell, Rupa Cousins, Stephanie Donegan, Michael Dunlop, Barry Dunlop, David Friedman, Edwene Gaines, Allen Klein, Christina Makrides, Sonia Milton, Rickie Moore, Maria Nemeth, Joe Nuckols, Leo Quinn, SQuire Rushnell, Christine Segal, Nicholas Tart, Marta Vago, Maggy Whitehouse, Barbara Winter.

I did not include their titles and the many books they've written, since I elaborate on all of that in the segments or Books in which their contributions appear in the upcoming pages. Along with Internet links for most of them to find out more about them.

To everyone involved in this transformative creation, my deeply felt gratitude and reverence. In one of the many ways **Moneylove 3.0** is different than other books, when I look over that list, I see not only contributors, and distinguished collaborators, but new and old friends, and it is a heartwarming experience indeed to know how much they gave of themselves and their wisdom to make this a unique and highly conscious effort.

Volume 1: The First 5 Books of Moneylove 3.0

CONTENTS

Instruction Manual for Moneylove 3.0

"Everyone is flailing through this life without an owner's manual, with whatever modicum of grace and good humor we can manage."

Anne Lamott

Yes, you've got it right, this is your Instruction Manual for **Moneylove 3.0.** It's part of my quest to make this the most powerful learning tool it can be, as well as the most unique book ever produced. And I certainly don't want any readers flailing through it.

Of course, if you're like me, you'll immediately put it away and go right to the heart of the matter, starting with the Introduction. I cannot count the number of instruction manuals I have ignored. You'd think this ignoring would be the last thing, and least sensible thing I would do, considering how technologically-challenged I am. Even my high tech electric toothbrush and toaster give me problems from time to time. That's when I go to the instruction manual, and it's often too late then.

So maybe instead of an instruction manual, I should call this a learning aid, or an explanation of how to get more out of what I have written. No, I think I'll stick with Instruction Manual and leave you to your own devices in terms of how seriously you consider reading it or discarding it. **Moneylove 3.0** will definitely work amazingly well without it. But I can also safely say that those who put the time and energy in to read it and actually put some of the strategies I suggest into practice, will notice more immediate and more satisfying results.

And because I wouldn't ask you to do anything I wouldn't do--I just bought a high tech USB microphone (whatever that is) and I am going to read the instruction manual word for word.

A Sign of My Respect for You

I am <u>not</u> writing what I believe is a first, an Instruction Manual for a book, because I think you are so stupid you need one to get through it all.

This is not an act of condescension, but a way I have of demonstrating my appreciation and respect for you. I am assuming you are the kind of person who has always read my books, my blog, listened to my audios, or attended my workshops--a smart, self-aware, and self-appreciating human being on a positive path forward in his or her life.

My intention was really to give some guidelines to those who are capable of making it much <u>more</u> than a book. I think there is more in this manual to do with where you go with all this <u>information</u> and <u>knowledge</u> and <u>wisdom</u> (three separate and distinct things as I am sure you know) to turn it into a continuing training, teaching, and inspirational source in your life after your first read-through. While I also know you are more self-motivating than most people out there, I still wanted to provide you with some tools to put into action, because I know you are the kind of person who wants to get every last drop of usefulness out of this, much as the eskimo uses every tiny part of the whale to improve his life.

A Clear Vision

I have a very clear vision of what i want to achieve and it's an ambitious one. I want you to immediately start using some of the suggestions to change every aspect of your life for the better. It's certainly not all about or just about money, though I would love to see you get rich. If you work at it and thus it works for you, then I cannot help but benefit. And I hope you have a clear vision of what you want to achieve.

I don't mean to insult you or myself, but we have not been keeping up. Moneylove 3.0 is about how to become more prosperous in a rapidly changing economy and happier in a rapidly changing world. presenting timeless principles in a new way to help you succeed in one of the most transformational periods in human history. Almost nothing is as we knew it ten or twenty years ago, and it would be impossible for any human being to have kept up with all the changes. Things have been moving so rapidly in technology, science, the economy, global relationships, and even social interaction that few people have had the time to step back, go inward, and reflect on exactly what the hell is happening--to the world, their work, and the people they once knew and loved.

My Contributors are Actually a Prosperity Faculty

One of the biggest ways in which this is a unique creation is in that I invited some of the authors, teachers, coaches, and mentors I most admire and have learned from to make major contributions in sharing their own thoughts and ideas on my subject. You will notice that their segments are sometimes unusually long. That's because I wanted you to be able to get as much of their good stuff as possible. For most of them, I have included a link to their website for more of what they offer.

There is enough information in Moneylove 3.0 to get you moving in the right direction. Human growth, elevation, enlightenment, and getting on the right path with passion and purpose, is a lifelong process. It's also a process that can be fun, exciting, filled with promise and conscious results. But the best way to do it is one step at a time, and many gifted teachers and coaches suggest those be baby steps.

Here is one way to go with all this that I think will be very effective:

1. **Read this entire volume.** By all means, when you enjoy a passage by one of my contributors, take a look at their website.
2. **Do the exercises and processes as you go along.** In addition to interviewing her extensively on her amazing grasp of the world of the Internet, I have borrowed and repeat frequently, Marianne Cantwell's admonition from her book, **How To Be A Free Range Human**, where she says: **Do the damn exercises!**
3. **Read it aloud, taking your time.** This is a powerful way to increase the power of any book you read offering new ideas about anything. It accesses a part of your brain that may not be reached by mere silent reading. Though you are welcome to find the best way to put this into practice, I suggest reading **Moneylove 3.0** all the way through first, then going back and reading one chapter/book at a time out loud. You can do this alone, but if you know someone, a friend or loved one, you think would appreciate a particular section, read it to them. You can even do this with distant friends via Skype or FaceTime. Or, you can record your reading it out loud and create your own audio book.

On to The Graduate School of Getting More Involved

And here are a few more suggestions I would call my graduate school program for those who have already finished reading all of **Moneylove 3.0**, and would like to make it more an individual experience.

1. Get a few of your friends or colleagues together and tell them several important ideas you've read and really like. You can make this a discussion group, and see if they can see the same useful ideas you chose working for them. I like Sonya Milton's statement, "I teach so that I can know."
2. Write a two-part essay on, "What is Right about Moneylove 3.0 and What Can Be Improved in Future Editions?" It would be highly unlikely that we exactly agree on every idea and point I've written or elicited from my contributors. The more you can make this your own creative venture, in terms of your individual desires and comfort level, the better it will work for you.
3. When you feel you have actually gotten desired results from putting at least one of my ideas into action, write and tell me about it. Obviously, I like getting emails of this sort, but it also will allow you to crystalize what value you received, and perhaps give you some thoughts on how to get even more for yourself from this work.
4. Each week for the next year, pick one sentence from one segment that will serve as your prosperity mantra for that week. It should be a sentence that speaks to you, that motivates or inspirits you. You can decide to post it on your wall, or add it to your computer's desktop, and to write it out or read it out loud as many times as you think will work best for you. But mostly, this is the sentence you will see as your mission statement for this particular week.

These exercises are not gimmicks, but rather ways you can make Moneylove 3.0 a more dynamic and powerful tool in your psychological arsenal. Give any or all of them a chance, and you will be amazed at how much more profoundly you will begin seeing changes in your results.

The sum, combined total of everything offered on the following pages, contains ideas and revelations that may surprise or even shock you. I do not come from a position that I am richer or smarter than you.

But I can pretty well declare that I've spent more time studying and learning this stuff than you have, and I have been unusually fortunate to attract teachers and mentors, some famous and some not, who have been the cream of the crop in terms of wisdom and coming up with practical solutions and inspiring ideas for living a life of true abundance and joy.

I've attempted to make this experience circular and permanent rather than linear and temporary. That is, I am laying down certain rules, principles, and ideas about prosperity that you can keep dipping into as you keep moving forward and upward in your life.

This is designed to be more simply functional than the way much information is presented today, zipping past our perceptions and cerebral cortexes faster than we can take it all in, and then disappearing as its forced out by the next new shiny thing.

This approach reflects my assertion that one of the new skills we all need moving forward in this new millennium (and so much has been happening so fast we sometimes forget it is a new millennium), one of the primary skills we all need to develop and keep honing is that of discernment, that of creating an inner editor to let the useful stuff in and keep the information overwhelm at bay. The new process about doing that inner editing, I call **The Law of Subtraction**, is presented in Book Three. It is a practical way to deal with what I have termed Information Asphyxiation.

I have talked a lot about this being unique in many different ways. One of those ways is that it is not meant to be at its most effective by the reader starting at page one and going through to the end, whether that takes days or weeks. For many people that would be a good idea, but if you are one of those readers, you should know that you are cheating yourself if that is it, if you just read it once cover to cover, and then put it aside.

This is an experience more than it is a book. The good thing about that is that it has no deadline, you don't have to return it to the library, you are not racing to prepare for a test. I'm sure as you looked over the table of contents, you saw some subjects that most interested you. This is not a volume for masochists, you don't have to punish yourself by reading stuff that isn't speaking to you right now just to get a few pages further along, you can go right to that section. So, again, if Time is your big issue, definitely read Book Five, **TimeLove** and its Appendix right away, before anything else (except perhaps this Instruction Manual and the Introduction--but even these are not mandatory).

One part of this volume, in particular, is not designed to be read all the way through all at once, and that is Book Eleven, **QuoteLove**. Even if you are overly ambitious, if you wanted to apply all 100 Quotercises to each of the 100 included quotes in turn, it could take months and miss the point of my approach to living. Take it nice and easy, don't stress or punish yourself. The section or Book is a resource, as many of the sections are, meant to be revisited time and again. It might be fun to take maybe five of the Quotercises and try them out. And if you find it a worthwhile and rewarding process, look forward to going back on a regular basis. This is a learning program, but you set your own schedule and your own choices. There's a lot here, and I don't want to regret including so much because some folks overdose and need medical care.

This all will work best for you if you begin it as an adventure, do the damn exercises, and have as much fun as you possibly can in the process.

Introduction

Is money your main objective in reading about prosperity consciousness? You might want to give that some additional thought.

In conversations with fellow prosperity thinkers and teachers, it has become evident that the concept of prosperity has dramatically broadened and expanded in the past twenty years. Perhaps we have come to realize the reality that money is just a part of it.

When college students were studied in the 1960s, 1970s, even into the 1990s, a majority said their main goal was to learn what they had to learn to make a lot of money out in the world. A much different answer emerges from the students in the 2000s. They want to find a career that excites their passion; they want to have a positive effect on the world; they want to keep learning and have fun, and money usually follows all these motivating factors. It is still important, but not as exclusively important as it once was.

And it isn't the top item offered when Silicon Valley companies, (or forward thinking companies in other parts of the world) are trying to hire bright young innovators. This is why so many of those companies have large recreational play areas on their campuses, and offer lots of interesting courses free to employees.

To put it another way, when a bunch of people were asked what their three wishes would be if a genie suddenly popped out of a lamp or bottle, very few of them listed money first, and some didn't even include it among the top three wishes. Health and a long and vital life were often picked, a happy life filled with lots of love was up there, being successful at something they really loved doing and that made a difference in the world came up often. Here's the point, I believe:

If you are happy and fulfilled, money is not very important, though there is no doubt money can smooth the

16

way on your path to happiness and fulfillment. A second part of the equation is that when you are happy and fulfilled, it is easier to create more money in your life. Other people are more attracted to you and want to buy whatever you are offering, be it a product, a service, or your valuable ideas.

Of course, money has a lot more significance in your life if you are worrying about the lack of it, or don't believe you deserve it or don't feel capable of producing it.

Though this book is based on many of the principles and concepts behind the writing of the successful 1978 book, **Moneylove**, very little from that book will be repeated here, except when I take a point from that book and greatly expand on it. Or when I use a quote from what I like to call **Moneylove 1.0** to illustrate an important idea in **Moneylove 3.0**--as I do now by repeating the first sentence from the Introduction of the 1978 version:

"You deserve to be rich, and you can be rich, **Moneylove** *can help you have a life of abundance, filled with love and creativity and, incidentally, all the cash you want."*

Now notice that right up front even back then, I made it clear that prosperity consciousness is not just about accumulating or even earning lots of money. Love and creativity come first, and "all the cash you want," is just a side effect of true prosperity thinking.

Edwene Gaines

My friend and one of my favorite prosperity teachers, Unity minister Edwene Gaines, puts it a slightly different way, saying:

"Prosperity for me is a healthy body, prosperity is relationships that are joyous and satisfying and intimate and honest and nurturing, and that work all the time.

Prosperity is work that we love so much that it's not work, it's play. And prosperity is all the money we can spend."

Not the Same Book, Not the Same Person

This is far from the book titled **Moneylove** that I wrote in 1978, which still has some solid and timeless perspectives on building prosperity consciousness and I am now far from the person I was in 1978.. (I now call that book, **Moneylove 1.0**.) We all live in a world that is far, far from the world we knew then. The changes have been dramatic and even traumatic, and your success in life (or lack of same) is largely due to how quick and nimble your reaction and adaptability and resilience have been during these sweeping changes. One of the changes that may have affected or concerned you on your path to a more prosperous life for you and your family is the

widening disparity between the richest and poorest of us. This is talked and written about a lot in this era of information overwhelm. However, chances are you are not at either of these extremes, but somewhere in the middle.

There is talk of the disappearing of the middle class. It hasn't gone anywhere, and in fact most of us are in it, certainly more people now exist between being really poor or really rich than did in 1978. But, as is often the case, all the talk, all the words expended in acknowledging and affirming the plight of the middle class, have only exacerbated the situation. Words are not actions, and little energy has been expended in dealing with the transformations that have taken place.

The changing workplace, changing economy, and changing world have often been blamed. The truth is there is more opportunity than catastrophe evident in all these changes. We've been caught up so intensely in the maelstrom of just trying to get by these changes, that we haven't taken the time to learn how to navigate them. As you'll soon discover, part of why I am more quick and nimble than many people, and certainly more so than most prosperity, motivational, and inspirational teachers, is that I was given time away from it all to study, reflect, meditate, and learn some profoundly new approaches to dealing with this changing world we live in.

In a very real sense, I was completely out of the workaday world, so I could think about what needed to be done and what needed to be taught once I was thrust back into action. I remember during my travails thinking, "This will either kill me or make me a much better teacher and writer."

A Conversation With My Readers

I want **Moneylove 3.0**, as was the 1978 book, to be like conversations I've had over the years with good friends who sometimes became my prosperity consciousness students, and in turn, even became my teachers and mentors. One was Louise Hay, whom I knew back in the days before she was a worldwide figure of inspiration. Louise more than repaid me for my prosperity coaching by saying when her book, "You Can Heal Your Life", came out and sold gazillions of copies, that "**Moneylove** is one of the best books on money."

Another was Jack Canfield, whom I first met in 1971 at a convention of The Association for Humanistic Psychology. I was a newsman for NBC Radio, covering the convention, and Jack was a bearded young workshop leader presenting a program called, *If Life Hands You a Lemon, Make Lemonade*. We became good friends and he and I co-led some Money and Self Esteem workshops. Jack was known as the expert on self-esteem, and I was being called "The Guru of Money."

One of the biggest laughs I ever got from an audience was from the prestigious Inside Edge leadership support group in Beverly Hills when I was introducing Jack and said, *"Jack has attended so many of my Moneylove seminars and I've attended so many of his self-esteem workshops that I now love myself a lot more than Jack loves himself, and he's a lot richer than I am."*

Book One The Foreplay of Success

Know what you want and learn how to ask for it.

Book Two Robust Expectations

Yes, I meant to write the preceding one sentence Book One!

There was a point to the brevity and it wasn't to shock or amuse you-though I did have fun doing it. The point I was making with a single sentence chapter/book is that this is perhaps the most essential part of getting what you want. AND:

It may not always be easy, but it is always this simple.

In the original 1978 book, **Moneylove**, I cited three essential elements to achieving one's desires:

1. **A Clear Vision of What You Want.**
2. **The Belief That You Will Get It.**
3. **Practical Skills to Put That Belief Into Action.**

This is still very much the clearest path to prosperity, but because it sometimes seems too simple or too glib, many people have ignored it. I have therefore distilled those three rules down to an even simpler formula of knowing what you want and being able to then ask for it. Jesus said, "Ask and ye shall receive." And many other prosperity teachers, philosophers, and spiritual masters have repeated the same simple truth. But with all of this wisdom, have you really taken it in?

I firmly, emphatically believe that knowing what you want is the one human quality that determines how successfully someone's life goes in terms of financial success, relationship success, health success, and creative success.

Members of other species only know very basic wants, such as food, shelter, security, and the desire to procreate. Most of these are instinctual. Only human beings possess a brain that can think about the future and exactly what will make it a happier and more fulfilling one.

Since writing the original **Moneylove**, I have learned even more about how prosperity consciousness works, and what tools and awarenesses bring people more of what they want. And Robust Expectations is one of the concepts that can set us humans apart in terms of satisfaction and accomplishment.

He Knew More Famous People Than Anyone

My first awareness of the term came in a conversation I had with my friend and mentor, the late Norman Cousins. Many people considered him a genius who had a major impact on the world. He led a distinguished career as longtime editor (30 years) of the prestigious Saturday Review, humanitarian and peace and nuclear disarmament activist who knew eight

U.S. Presidents and often went on diplomatic peace missions for them.

Norman also knew many of the world's most famous and successful people in the arts, science, entertainment, religion--a cornucopia of the movers and shakers of the 20th Century. and he counted among his friends both Albert Einstein and Albert Schweitzer. He was also the bestselling author of Anatomy of An Illness. As I said in my Introduction, this led to the science of psychoneuroimmunology, but he is also considered the father of laughter therapy. For me, one of his most amazing accomplishments was becoming a popular and prominent member of the medical faculty at UCLA without ever having had medical training.

A Common Quality of The Great and Famous

The conversation I refer to came in 1980, as I was preparing my book, **Psychological Immortality**. I asked Norman whether there was any one single quality that the most successful, most acknowledged, and most fulfilled people he had known had in common.

I said:

"Norman, you know more famous and accomplished and happily fulfilled self-actualized people than anyone I can think of. Is there a common denominator, some quality they all shared that may have contributed to their great success, their profound impact on the world?"

Norman thought for a moment, and then said:

"Yes, yes, there is a common denominator for all of these great men and women: They each woke up almost every morning of their lives with <u>robust expectations</u>."

I don't really know if he had ever used that term before, or whether my very simple question triggered it for the first time. What matters to me is that those two words changed my life, and I suggest they could change yours as well

Ever since that phrase came from his lips, it has bounced around in my consciousness and become a personal quest of mine to achieve, at least as much as possible. Most days I am successful in doing it, and this was true even during my 12 years in prison. I began using that term as my personal mantra, a marker that would let me know when I was on the right path and tuned into my highest purpose in life.

Robust expectations doesn't just involve an attitude shift, but a determination to create things to be robustly expectant about in your life.

Norman Cousins certainly walked his talk, and often said that as a young boy he *"set out to discover exuberance."*

The word "robust" is defined as meaning strong and healthy, vigorous, powerful, durable, resilient, long-lasting, and not likely to fail or weaken.

The word "expectation" is defined as a strong belief that something will happen or be the case in the future.

Note the use of the word "belief," meaning you don't necessarily have to have factual proof that positive expectations will actually occur in order for them to benefit your emotional attitude. And you can have robust expectations about something wonderful happening in your near future without being specific. However, specificity is good, too.

I, for instance, have robust expectations that **Moneylove 3.0** will exceed even the two million copies sold of the original 1978 book (mostly in paperback and over a 25-year period.) My robust expectations are also that it won't take a full generation to achieve this level of success.

It Works With Or Without Getting What You Want

Now, here's the remarkable part of all of this: it doesn't have to happen in order for me to achieve the benefits of the energy and confidence inherent in this robust expectation. If the book falls short of that goal, it is merely a temporary setback, and its impact will affect me only for a fraction of the time my preceding robust expectations have.

Those celebrated people who Norman Cousins said woke up every day with robust expectations did not always receive a positive response to those expectations. What mattered was their resilience when something didn't turn out the way they wanted, so that they got back to having robust expectations about a new effort in the same direction, or perhaps coming up with a completely new robust expectation.

For me, robust expectations involve having an excited and optimistic anticipation for what lies ahead. Not everything I look forward to turns out the way I would like it to, but I am always juggling so many balls of positive expectation in the air that even when one falls to the ground, there are enough left to keep things in motion.

I don't think it has to be a grand result you are expecting. It can be something small, like a positive response to a favor you asked of a friend (and, by the way, having robust expectations before you ask for the favor can affect the energy and enthusiasm with which you ask). It does take mental discipline to know what you want, to have that clear vision of it, and to have the belief and skills to put it into action. This often just means knowing how and who to ask, but robust expectations give it a whole new, expanded dimension.

Brian Tracy on Expectations

As motivational author and speaker, Brian Tracy, says, *"Winners make a habit of manufacturing their own positive expectations in advance of the event."*

For me "robust expectations" seems a much more powerful phrase than "positive expectations." Robust is a word that seems to have its own vitality, its own charged energy, while positive is a greatly overused word that doesn't register with nearly as much impact.

Low Expectations Can Mean Low Results

Don't buy into all the self-help authors and well-meaning advice givers who tell you to keep your expectations low so you won't be disappointed. As I lay on a prison bunk and imagined that I had written a bestselling book and was being interviewed by Oprah Winfrey about it, and telling her how well I overcame the negative aspects and terrible physical environment of prison life, it affected my mood in that moment.

I wasn't thinking about whether this was a realistic expectation or not. It seemed a possibility however, because I was planning to go back to writing books, and I had actually been an Oprah guest for my 1984 book, **Men on Women**, when she was a local talk show host in Chicago with everyone predicting she would be the next big thing on national TV

Since my release, it hasn't happened, at least not yet, and Oprah doesn't have the same network show with its immense audience that she had back then. But it doesn't matter, because I already received hours of energy and satisfaction picturing it in my mind. And those robust expectations helped me decide exactly how I wanted my years in prison to turn out, if only so I could entertain and inspire people who heard my story. It helped me decide and declare what I wanted, to go back to the content of Book One.

Robust Expectations Are Ones You Make Happen

It is important to make the distinction that the expectations I describe as robust are not things that happen to you, but things you make happen. Yes, we're talking about optimism, but in a very specific and powerful way. I took it a step further by deciding that we can have the intention to create this state of mind. We can plan for it, we can plant seeds to achieve it, and we can maximize its positive effects on the way our lives turn out. I will share some of the ways I have discovered to do this. And hopefully, you've started to have some robust expectations yourself of what is coming up in the rest of this book.

More from Norman Cousins

Here are some additional thoughts Norman Cousins shared with me during our many conversations that he kindly let me record. I used this in **Psychology Immortality**, though I'm not sure that I completely understood how powerful a statement it was at the time Norman said it:

"I have learned never to underestimate the capacity of the human mind and body to regenerate--even when the prospects seem most wretched. The life-force may be the least understood force on earth. William James said that human beings tend to live too far within self-imposed limits. It is possible that these limits will recede when we respect more fully the natural drive of the human mind and body toward perfectibility and regeneration. Protecting and cherishing that natural drive may well represent the finest exercise of human freedom."

For me, this capacity of the human mind and body to regenerate and become more perfect is demonstrated in creating situations that will produce robust expectations under any circumstances, in Norman Cousins' words, even when the prospects "seem most wretched." We are all sometimes faced with dire circumstances, like major illness, losing a job or loved one, being in prison, having a major project fail. We can escape much of the fear, anxiety, and pain by focusing our attention and having the intention to look forward to something good with a lot of

28

emotion-backed anticipation. In other words, robust expectations.

My Romantic Robust Expectations

Long before I met Norman Cousins, even before he wrote **Anatomy of an Illness**, I had my own experience of the power of robust expectations. I've told this story a few times over the years, but as I explore the powerful impact creating robust expectations has had on me, I realize even more what an amazing life lesson occurred in my early years while I was in army basic training at Fort Knox, Kentucky.

I was very inexperienced and shy around women, though I would never have admitted I was still a virgin at 21. Before I went into the army, I took an inexpensive one week Caribbean cruise out of Miami with my cousin Steve. It was a pretty dinky ship called the S.S. Evangeline, and the total cost for one week was $149. The cabins were so small, you could sit on your bunk with the door open and touch the opposite wall of the outside hall.

On the cruise, I spent a lot of time with Sharon, a very sweet and pretty girl from Mobile, Alabama. In those more innocent times, our activity was mostly kissing, which we both enjoyed immensely. So much so, we made plans to spend a weekend in Nashville, about the halfway point between Ft. Knox and Mobile, during the weekend pass I would get at the end of basic training.

About two weeks before our weekend came the most dreaded and grueling part of basic training, the 30 mile march with a full 75 pound pack, and including the walk up Agony Hill. I would have to admit that though we had done a lot of running and calisthenics in basic training, I was not in as good shape as most of my fellow recruits. But when we staggered back into our barracks at the end of that march, I was the only one who was not exhausted, and as far as I could tell, the only one whose feet were not bleeding or covered with blisters.

I owe it all to Sharon from Mobile, and my robust expectations of our weekend together. You see, I was not really on that march at all, at least my mind, and more importantly my imagination were not there suffering through the rough physical challenge it took to keep going. I was in Nashville. making out with Sharon. I'm sure my brain was oozing lots of endorphins during the march, and probably a few hormones came into play as well.

My robust expectations of my romantic weekend with Sharon kept me going, kept me free of many of the negative effects others felt from the ordeal. And I have since realized another vital part of this whole episode. You see, when I got to Nashville, with a friend from my basic training unit (Sharon was bringing her cute girlfriend Kay along for him.), Sharon was not in a very romantic mood. The weekend did not meet any of my fantasy expectations. But that didn't take away one single thing from the amazing march I wasn't really there for because of Sharon.

It's only years afterwards that I realized that the impact of robust expectations can produce great positive results even if the expectations are not met, aren't in fact nearly as good as you imagined they would be. I would go so far as to say that the act of having the robust expectations is more important than realizing them, of having them come true. Especially on a consistent, daily basis.

Unrealistic Expectations

A note here. Back in the beginning of what was called the Human Potential Movement, or Humanistic Psychology in the 1970s, a lot of attention was focused on the danger to emotional well-being and relationships of having what were commonly called Unrealistic Expectations. And it is true that having an expectation that is unbalanced on the side of fantasy with little chance of actually happening can be destructive, and may even be at the root of many relationship and other failures.

Whats an example of an unrealistic expectation? Well relationship expert, Joe Tanenbaum, author of Male and Female Realities, used one I really thought vividly shed light on the issue. He said that if a woman expects a man to be as easily willing and able to share his feelings as she is, it would be like expecting your poodle to have all your phone messages ready for you when you got home. In other words, because men are wired differently than women, this would be an unrealistic expectation and doomed to failure.

Wise Words from Ilana Rubenfeld

My friend and famed Gestalt therapist and bodywork pioneer, Ilana Rubenfeld, came up with another good reason to be cautious about expectations. She told me that she felt the number one reason many relationships fail is that *"people fall in love with potential rather than who the other person is right now. Thus, they end up being a parent, teacher, or therapist for the other person rather than an equal loving partner."* She went on to say, *"If you are not willing to fall in love with someone who has already reached much of their potential, you are probably not ready to receive love."* That absolutely affected my relationship life, and who I might choose to be involved with, not only in romantic relationships, but in friendships and business connections.

Ilana Rubenfeld also pointed out that this other person may indeed have great potential which they may or may not realize, but they should still be judged on the basis of what they have achieved or become up to the moment you met them.

I have found that people who have already achieved or accomplished something worthwhile in their lives usually have a lot more future potential than those who haven't done much personal growing, learning, or prospering.

I am suggesting that any robust expectations have a foundation of reality, of something that is very possible to have or accomplish.

In terms of relationships, I was once very attracted to a beautiful and brilliant woman who told me at our first meeting, "I'm not really into relationships. They never seem to work out well for me." Like many a dewy-eyed male before me, I ignored this statement and the history of failed relationships she eventually revealed to me. Sure enough, in less than a year, our relationship collapsed as she just wasn't ready for that kind of commitment. I guess my hopeful expectations of our being together forever could have been called "robust," but they were based on an unlikely outcome that went against both her belief and her history.

I cannot stress enough how vital it is to the whole process to not have to suspend belief in order to focus on your robust expectations.

A Major Building Block

I strongly believe and assert that developing the ability to create and nurture robust expectations in your life can be a major building block in the foundation of all your future prosperity and success. And I don't mean only as an inner ally for your building of wealth. It can dramatically impact the way you present yourself to others. We get most of our money from other people who buy our goods, services, ideas and creative skills. The more they find you interesting, attractive, and confident, the more they will want to give you their money. But they also will want to give you their love and support.

People who have robust expectations usually have successful relationships, solid friendships, a lot of recognition and acknowledgment from others, and end up making a worthwhile and important impact on the world. They also may very well live longer.

Robust Expectations Can Extend Your Life

I've mentioned that I first heard the term when talking to Norman Cousins about my book, **Psychological Immortality:** *Using Your Mind To Extend Your Life.* Norman described the power of robust expectations to stave off death itself:

"You can have people who are ill with malignancies which might be expected to claim their lives after three or four months, but these people are determined to live through, say a fortieth wedding anniversary or a 70th birthday, or whatever...and they do."

People do seem to live beyond normal expectations when an important event is approaching. Dr. Phillip R. Kunz of Brigham Young University conducted a survey of 746 subjects. They all had died, as he got their names from obituary columns. He compared their dates of death with their birthdays and found that 46% of the deaths occurred in the three-month period following their birthdays. This indicated that these people were able to postpone death by looking forward to their birthdays. Only 8% died in the three months before their birthday.

Obviously, for a large proportion of these people, the desire to celebrate one more birthday kept them alive. Dr. H. Keith Fischer, who was a Clinical Professor of Psychiatry at Temple University, believed that will power was very much involved in this phenomenon and that people set up what he called "Emotionally Invested Deadlines"--special dates they want to live to observe, special events they want to participate in, such as a grandchild's birth or wedding or a long-planned vacation trip. How many times have we heard a grandparent say, "I want to live to see you married?" And I couldn't help but note as I was doing the final edit on this work, former three term New York governor, Mario Cuomo, died at 82 on the very same day his son, Andrew, was sworn in for his second term as governor.

This idea of "emotionally invested deadlines" (which sounds like robust expectations to me!) isn't new, nor is the evidence: John Adams and Thomas Jefferson, both signers of the Declaration of Independence, died on the 50th anniversary of its adoption.

One prominent physician told me that the best way to support and increase longevity is to give people something important to look forward to. Many doctors have reported that patients have held on against tremendous odds waiting for the arrival of a loved one from a far distance. In fact, this was true in the case of my own father, who not only stayed alive an extra day awaiting my arrival from out-of-state, but snapped out of a comatose state just long enough to exchange a few words with me.

I only relate that robust expectations can help someone defy death itself to illustrate the awesome power that is available to all of us. If that power can do this, imagine what it can do if you harness it in pursuit of your dreams.

These expectations are a separate event in your life, separate from the achieving or non-achieving of the result you expect or hope for. Remember the definition I talked about at the beginning of this book, the act of expecting. This is a different event from the act of receiving or not receiving what you want or expect. You can thrive on the energy created by robust expectations for some time, and get over any disappointing results very quickly. This is part of one of the most valuable attributes we can have as human beings, resilience--the ability to bounce back quickly and move forward in our lives. Or as the Merriam Webster dictionary puts it: "an ability to recover from or adjust easily to misfortune or change."

One significant factor I would keep in mind as you decide what, if anything, of this tool you can use in your life. Whenever we have a target in our sights that we want to hit sometime in the future, a mark we want to reach, an aspiration we want to achieve--whether it's financial success, creative fulfillment, more love, better health, a more interesting and fulfilling life--our true desire goes beyond that specific goal. What I have found over many years of studying human accomplishment is that people want to have a certain feeling they imagine they will have if they are successful in achieving their desire or goal.

In Moneylove programs over the years, I have stressed that it isn't the million dollars you want, but rather that feeling you associate with being a millionaire. And the amazing and wonderful truth is that you can start having that feeling before the money even begins to come in. Realizing this can add to the whole robust expectations experience.

Moneylove Action Exercise

An exercise you might try right now is to pick a specific goal you have, let's say something you would like to have or accomplish within the next year. Now picture how reaching that goal will make you feel. You can take it further by deciding to pretend, maybe for the next 24 hours, that you feel that way right now. Just see what happens. And check out whether you can actually create some of that same feeling by putting more energy into having robust expectations of getting to that target, hitting that bullseye, succeeding in that effort and realizing that dream.

What gives robust expectations their power is the fact that you have taken some action in the direction of achieving that particular want or desire. This gives your expectation its robustness and aliveness, and gives you the energy to get there more easily.

You May be Underutilizing a Major Asset

As I have talked to people over the years, whether in coaching sessions, during seminars, or just in conversation, I have discovered one thing. Most of them--and I include myself in this--underutilize a very powerful mental/emotional/spiritual capacity of the human brain, the ability to daydream, the power to pretend and visualize and even to clearly see what we really want. Too many of us put too much time into left brain activities like planning, organizing, working long hours. We avoid or ignore right brain activities like daydreaming, meditating, reflecting, and leaving time and space in our lives for new realizations, new adventures, and new directions to emerge and evolve.

Study after study has shown that creative people use their right brain more than their left brain. What I believe is that like any unused muscle, you can exercise and train your right brain to deliver more of the good stuff it specializes in. I understand that there is new scientific research indicating that the left brain, right brain dichotomy is inaccurate. that both sides are usually actively engaged. However, I'll continue to use these terms, because most people relate to them and know what you mean by saying left brain activity or right brain activity.

And just because someone has spent his or her whole life using more of their intellectual, analytical left brain, doesn't mean they can't start developing right brain skills. We all have a whole brain, and whether by following in our parents' footsteps, or just by having put more attention on our left brain, doesn't mean we can't switch focus. It takes

36

practice, like developing any new skill, but it is certainly worth exploring. Conversely, some folks might be so totally focused on their emotional, spiritual, imaginative side, that they would benefit by developing more left-brain skills.

When doing seminars for specific groups, I have noticed very powerful differences in responses, questions, and enthusiasm for what I am teaching between, say a group of psychiatrists or lawyers or engineers, and groups of writers, musicians, actors and other creative artists. Through their training and personal inclinations, each of these groups has learned to operate in a certain way and develop certain mental skills. It's always been a puzzle to me that we don't try to differentiate between left brain thinkers and right brain thinkers when we communicate with a broader audience. I get responses to my books, audios and workshops from both groups, and those responses are definitely different. They absolutely take my information from different perspectives, and like very different things about what I write or say.

What I Have Observed in Panama

Though this may be judgmental on my part, I have a strong feeling that the country I now call home, Panama, like many countries in Latin America, is somewhat lacking in left brain focus. This is evident in the primitive aspects of systems, both governmental and legal, of organizations, and of the basic rules people live by.

The Panamanian people are very right-brained in the way they deal with adversity, in their warmth, in their ability to shake off misfortune to a salsa beat. A basic mantra of life here is: "tomorrow, (or mañana) is another day and most likely will be a better one." The degree to which a visitor or expat living here is frustrated by this is exactly the degree to which that person is, as they say, stuck inside his or her own head. That being said, I have to admit that I have not yet met anyone who was not born here who does not say that the culture underlying life in Panama doesn't sometimes drive them crazy. When making this point, I feel it's only fair to point out that Panama consistently makes the top ten list on surveys of which countries have the happiest citizens.

Resilience Muscle

A powerful aspect to developing more robust expectations in your life is the fact that it will be exercising and training your resilience muscle, giving you more practice in bouncing back under more favorable circumstances. It was easier for me to bounce back after not having that wonderful romantic weekend with Sharon in Nashville, since I had already had the amazing experience of just floating through my thirty mile march as I anticipated the weekend. The final results did not negate the time spent enjoying the robust expectations.

A Psychological Arsenal

I often get complimented on my resilience in circumstances others might find daunting or debilitating I strongly believe my always having upcoming events for which I have robust expectations contributes greatly to this part of my psychological arsenal.

By the way, this is a new term I recently came up with: psychological arsenal. It describes those tools we adopt and use to keep our equilibrium in this world now filled with rapid-fire change and challenges. It is almost like a constant state of war. With so many negative people, and inaccurate and overwhelming information bombarding us on a daily basis, we need an arsenal of healthy emotional weapons to survive and thrive so we are not in a constant state of victimhood with the feeling that we are living in enemy territory.

Weapons of Mass Distraction

Among the ammunition I have had in my arsenal for a very long time is the fact that I can lose myself in a good mystery novel. I have always made it a habit of having at least three or four available, though they now reside in my Kindle rather than on a shelf.

Here's a major part of my arsenal that I came to appreciate more and more after writing a book called, **FRIENDS:** *The Power and Potential of the Company You Keep.* I have a few good friends whom I can Skype or video call with FaceTime if I am troubled or undecided or just need to get a lift from human contact. I also have a few such friends here in Panama, who can join me for lunch or dinner when I am in the mood for good company.

A third weapon of mass distraction is to always have some of my favorite comfort food ready in case I need help getting past overwhelm or disappointment. In my freezer right now are several bags of bagels and a large package of smoked salmon. I also have an emergency supply of See's chocolate lollipops, and a package of one of my guilty pleasures, Stouffer's Stuffed Pepper, which is ridiculously overpriced in my local supermarket as it has to be imported from the U.S.

Settling in a new country and living in an apartment that doesn't permit animals makes me miss having a cat. The four cats over thirty-some years of my life added lots of companionship and many moments of hilarity. They are all greatly missed. A dog or cat can be a major component of any psychological arsenal. And, of course, a relationship partner or spouse can provide much in the way of loving support to anyone. I am now choosing to live alone, but I am willing to consider changing that status should the right candidate with smiling eyes show up. I offer seven powerful **Weapons of Mass Distraction** in Book Twelve, the final segment of this work.

I want to provide some specific suggestions for intentionally building upcoming events in your life that can produce these robust expectations or bursts of positive and healing energy. You can probably come up with your own events, perhaps even better suited to your individual needs and talents.

Moneylove Action Exercises

TEN THINGS YOU CAN DO TO CREATE SOME NEW ROBUST EXPECTATIONS IN YOUR LIFE:

1. Generate some form of creative effort that could get you a very satisfying result and effect extra momentum and even cash in your life.

As a writer, I get this one going every time I send out some article or book proposal to a potential publisher. Chances are you have some special knowledge in some area, and especially with the Internet today, you can deliver it pretty effortlessly to several sites that publish this kind of information and will pay for it. Or maybe you write poetry or fiction. It doesn't have to have the potential of earning you a fortune for you to have robust expectations about it being accepted for publication.

In prison, I developed a number of strategies and formulas for myself,

designed to help me keep growing in emotionally healthy ways despite the unhealthy constant of negative events and comments surrounding me. One of these was to make an effort, on any given day, to have several things I was looking forward to with robust expectations.

These could be small or large expectations, things that were imminent or scheduled to happen at some point in the future. I found that I could set myself up for robust expectations by putting certain things in motion which could produce positive results.

Writing my cartoon gags created a sequential series of such anticipatory sensations. I would create twenty or so cartoon scenes and captions for each of my cartoonists, and send them off. I would then be able to look forward to hearing from the artists in a week or two as to whether any of them liked any of my twenty gags enough to draw them up and submit them to magazines. The artist might like anywhere from one to five of the gags. By the way, in each batch of gags, I had one or two favorites, ones I thought were guaranteed winners. Rarely did those get

chosen by the cartoonist. This amused me, because they took other gags I thought were less funny and often sold them. I wasn't disappointed that my robust expectations about my favorite gags were almost never realized. There were usually lots of second tier gags that were accepted. After celebrating this, I then could look forward to a magazine actually buying some of them. If this happened, I could then look forward to eventually getting my 25% share of the sale from the cartoonist.

Once I heard a sale had been made, I always had at least one item in the canteen that I was looking forward to buying with my gag money, and I could have robust expectations about getting it as soon as the check arrived. Gagwriting is not a lucrative career. My average income was from $50 to $150 a month. In prison, however, that was an abundant amount. The average prison job paid about $18 a month for a forty hour week. I was that rare prison inmate who was self-supporting, something else to celebrate.

This form of robust expectations was vital for my time in prison to be more a positive than a terribly negative experience. In a place that offered me little or no acknowledgment of my value as a human being, it was an affirmation that I still had a viable and even marketable sense of humor, which was priceless.

What can you produce that someone else will pay money for, or give you some satisfying acknowledgement for? Find an area you are talented or knowledgeable in, and give it a try. And remember, the robust expectations you have are still impacting your consciousness even if you're not successful in having your product or service or ideas accepted.

2. **Plan a trip to some totally new place.** It doesn't have to be far away or of long duration. If there is literature available online, study it and generate a sense of excitement about visiting this spot. Plan for your trip a month from now and you can enjoy a whole month of robust expectations.

3. **Try a new menu item at a restaurant.** Most good restaurants have their menus on their websites now, and there are lots of review sites for restaurants, so you can choose something other people have raved about. I usually do this once a week, though granted it is easier to find something I have never tasted before now that I'm living in Panama. Just the other day, I tried a new drink called Avena juice, made from oats. It was sweet, but not too sweet and delicious, so now I have robust

expectations of having it again, and maybe even learning how to make it at home.

4. **Find someone in your old address books or your memory banks whose company you really enjoyed in the past, but whom you** haven't been in

touch with for years. Make an effort to reconnect with them (one of the great aspects of sites like Facebook). This can provide lots of robust expectations, and even if you are nervous about contacting them after so long, that can be a wake-up booster shot to your imagination.

5. **Revisit some activity or place you really got a lot of positive experiences from, but you haven't done or been to in a long time.** For me, it has been over 20 years since I've played tennis, which I will be doing one day soon. And I have robust expectations about this, even though I haven't set a date for my return to the game.

6. **Sign up to learn some new skill or activity you think will be fun, even if you have no idea if you can do well at it.** This is one of the reasons I am planning to sign up for Salsa lessons. I'm now living in Central America, so there will be lots of opportunities to practice.

7. **Plan to, at some certain date, tell someone you've been close to something you feel about them that is positive.** It could be as simple as telling an old friend you love him or her. Or maybe relate a time when their friendship was really important to you and you never let them know exactly how important. The great thing about this exercise is that it not only gives you a chance to have robust expectations about what you're going to tell them, and about their reaction, but there is an excellent chance the experience itself will expand the connection between the two of you once you reveal to them. And maybe you can even have robust expectations about their turning around and telling you something you didn't know about their feelings about

you.

8. **Make a positive change of some kind in your life.** Perhaps start some kind of exercise regimen, or change your diet in some positive way, or organize your closet, or give yourself a total spa experience. Or, if you don't now get regular massages, start getting at least one a week.

Your robust expectations in this instance can be about enjoying the process and also about how this change will impact your life.

9. **Find a new place in your space to spend time.** This can be a consciousness-altering experience as most people do tend to favor one room in their living space, and hardly spend any time at all in the rest of the house or apartment. You can have robust expectations about the advantage of doing this, and actually doing it can give you some new perspectives on what is important to you about the space you inhabit. I have been exploring taking my computer out to the little courtyard outside my apartment door and doing some of my writing there. These changes seem to stimulate new energy for me and are certainly worthy of having robust expectations about.

10. **Finally, strategy number ten: Have robust expectations starting right now about the positive effects you will be getting by adding this whole concept of robustly expecting some new things and positive changes in your life from now on.**

One thing that will add to any and all of these specific action exercises is the amount of emotional amplitude you put into them, or maybe we should call it "robust expectation amplitude."

In other words, the more of your own emotional energy you put into the anticipation of something coming up in your life, the more powerful a tool it will be to energize and motivate you in other areas of your life.

Passion Needs Reality

We hear a lot nowadays about how important it is to have lots of passion in our lives--passion for what we do, passion for what we create, passion for the way we live our lives. But for passion to really deliver everything we want and need, everything we are willing to deserve, that passion needs a partner. That passion needs to be reality-based in robust expectations that will carry us to our goal.

Let me use a simplistic example. Suppose you have met someone with whom you would like a passionate relationship. You want to be with that person and the passion, the emotional energy you devote to the pursuit of your goal is important. But unless you can actually believe you can achieve that relationship, unless you can generate robust expectations that you will win your heart's desire, the passion won't take you anywhere.

Also, if you have something you are looking forward to with great emotional energy, it is always useful to have some idea of what the next big thing will be that you will be looking forward to. I was really impressed with something one of the seven original American astronauts, Wally Schirra, told me in the green room at a Denver TV station, where we were both scheduled to promote our books. He was retired from the space program in in private business. He said he loved what he was doing and always had expected to go into business when he retired from space exploration. He said people would come up to him and express astonishment that he could be so happy doing something that seemed so less exciting than being an astronaut. Wally told me it was his father who told him that whenever he was doing something that he was passionate about, he should still always have in mind what he would like to do next. Again, Robust Expectations.

Of course, you can have several things you are anticipating with robust expectations. I am always aware of the things and projects I may have put on the back burner until I have the time and space in my life to focus on them. These are all worthy of robust expectations, and this includes several book ideas. More about the back burner in Book Twelve, **Weapons of Mass Distraction.**

The Robust Expectation of Learning Spanish

It also useful to have one project or major aspiration in life that keeps on giving in terms of robust expectations, and has a relatively long life. For me, this is learning Spanish.

I am really excitedly looking forward to the point when I can converse with non-English-speaking Panamanians. But even after that desire is fulfilled, I plan to keep learning until I can eventually do a motivational talk in Spanish, or even a stand-up comedy act. I hope to have enough of a command of the language to be able to master the nuances necessary to say something funny in Spanish and get a laugh.

It will be an ongoing series of revelations, from the point where I hear and understand what people around me are saying, to the point where I can have a flirtatious chat with a beautiful Latina woman, or negotiate a good price on something I want to buy, or manage to do something like order high speed Internet, or have a conversation with an acupuncturist I heard was very good but only speaks Mandarin and Spanish.

And then there will come the day when all my expectativas roboostas will be anticipated in español.

There are two personal points I want to make. First, I have not been as diligent in learning Spanish as I could have been, and thus have been a slow learner. In a strange way, this is beneficial as it lets my robust expectations last longer. The other point is that one of the reasons I am determined to learn another language is because of all the studies showing the positive effects on the brain and memory of doing so.

Since this all started with Norman Cousins, I'll give you two quotes from him that are relevant to the subject.

First, *"The capacity for hope is the most significant fact of life. It provides human beings with a sense of destination and the energy to get started."*

And something that makes me want to add how vital it is that your robust expectations be for positive happenings in your life, and how magically this will banish some of your anxiety, fears, and worrying about something in the future that most likely will never happen. Norman Cousins said:

"People are never more insecure than when they become obsessed with their fears at the expense of their dreams."

Instead of obsessed, I'll say that you should become intensely focused on your dreams at the expense of your fears.

From My Prison Journals on Robust Expectations

Here's a thought from my prison journals, which will form a major part of my future book on that experience, in which robust expectations played a huge part. I wrote this in 2000:

I woke up this Saturday morning thinking about strength of character--congratulating myself on how much of it I must have in order to so triumphantly endure this living example of pervasive barbarism known as prison. I wrote some cartoon gags, and tried to remember a dream I had, thinking I had to finish reading All About Dreams, so as to learn how to remember them more vividly. I also had some things to share in this journal and it dawned on me that this was starting out like the kind of wake-up-day-full-of-lots-ofinteresting-things-to-do that I had often experienced on the outside. The kind of getting-up-with-a-smile-on-my-face morning I now often have here in my tiny cell.

This made me realize I was waking up more often than not with "robust expectations." I had the thought that it takes a whole lot of strength of character to wake up in here with robust expectations. But I also recognized something I haven't been that willing to acknowledge in my life, that I have hardly ever taken full advantage of this capacity I have to triumph over difficult challenges. If I can handle this so well, what other great challenges could I have handled in my life that I never took on? I could have attempted so much more, used so much more of whatever is getting me through this so easily. This is a truth that is not only my own, but one that every human being

shares--that we have to own up to the fact that we were built to handle much more than we have ever taken on.

In more personal terms, robust expectations means for me, having an exuberant anticipation for what lies ahead.

Think back to some time in your own life when you were really excited over something that was about to happen, some positive event in your life you were absolutely certain was coming. Chances are your emotions were soaring, and you found the mundane discomforts and annoyances of daily life a lot less so. You possibly felt as if you were defying gravity itself. In a way, you were. Emotional gravity. As your spirits become lighter than air with robust expectations, they take off.

The anticipatory tingle of robust expectations is a vital component of everything good and special in life, from creating something worthwhile to falling in love.

Three Daily Robust Expectations

One of my own formulas for success is believe that a day is good when I have at least three things to look forward to in my life. These can be big or small events. At the moment I am writing this, I am looking forward to the release of this book online, and what I robustly expect will be an enthusiastic reception by readers. Also, I am meeting a friend for a favorite breakfast at Manolo's Cafe here in Panama City, Panama. We'll sit at a patio table and I will order the bacon omelet, with bacon on the side, or "tocino en el lado" the very first Spanish phrase I learned after moving here. This is a great spot for people-watching, and a lot of those people are exceptionally beautiful women. My third item creating an anticipatory tingle is reading a bit more of a book on my Kindle, a mystery novel about

Sherlock Holmes and his wife, Mary, as created in the series by Laurie R. King.

None of these three robust expectations will fill my whole day or change my life, but they will provide a great start so that I enter the day with energy and enthusiasm and the strength to handle anything that happens.

Still More from Norman Cousins

More than most people, Norman Cousins thought about the essential qualities of life and what it meant to be a human being, as well as finding out new things about the capacity of the human brain. In his book, **Celebration of Life**, he said:

"Humans are not helpless. They have never been helpless. They have only been deflected or deceived or dispirited. This is not to say their history has not been pockmarked by failure. But failure is not the ultimate fact of life; it is an aspect of life in which transient or poor judgments play larger roles than they ought to. So long as people do not persuade themselves they are creatures of failure; so long as they have a vision of life as it ought to be; so long as they comprehend the full meaning and power of the unfettered mind--so long as this is so--they can look at the world and, beyond that, at the universe, with the sense that they can be unafraid of their fellow humans and can face choices not with dread but with great expectations."

As someone who actually experienced fetters (the manacles around one's ankles often used when transporting inmates to a new prison or to an outside medical facility for treatment), I fell in love with Norman's phrase, "The full meaning and power of the unfettered mind." It goes along with my assertion that many people have minds imprisoned by fear, old habits and behaviors, and old negative programming. What a noble and majestic aspiration it can be to unfetter our minds!

How's your day looking so far, and can you come up with a simple and easy robust expectation for tomorrow? I certainly have the robust expectation that you can and will.

Book Three The Law of Subtraction

The mind takes its shape from what it holds, and therefore, Zen-like, sometimes grows more graceful because of what it has kept out. Lance Morrow, TIME

I have no doubt that this single sixteen-page book in this library of prosperity may be the most important one for many readers. Of course, I could say this about any of the segments, chapters, or books, or whatever designation appeals to you most. In any event, one subject or another may be the torch to light your inner flame, the trigger to set you off on a clearer and more productive path. As I suggested in the opening Instruction Manual, it's up to you to decide, to judge, to conclude which is the most relevant and exciting part for you right now. Just don't leave it at that, embrace it and study it and put its ideas and strategies into immediate use.

I mention this, because part of this being totally different from anything you've read before, is the fact that I used my own techniques to write it. The Law of Subtraction figured prominently in that process. Because it is about choosing your information, using your free will to decide what is valuable to take in and important to leave out. If information overload is a major issue for you, then you may as well start right here. But don't be defined or constricted by cultural habits that dictate you start at the beginning of any book and go straight through to the end, not paying attention to what your inner knowing tells you is the essential part for you to read first.

A Confession

And I'll make a confession here that few writers would be willing to make. As I decided which areas of prosperity consciousness I wanted to cover, and created the

63 twelve main focal points, I had no idea what order they belonged in. The current order works for me, but may not for you. This is your learning tool, and you are the decider as to which subjects should be your majors on this journey, and which your minors.

There is just so much junk mail for the mind out there, especially online. Much of it ought to have a warning posted:

Danger!

Taking This Into Your Mind
May be Hazardous to your
Mental, Emotional, Spiritual
and Even Physical Well-being

My mentor for this concept and this chapter is Sherlock Holmes. Nothing I had ever read before impressed itself upon my twelve-year-old mind as this passage from **A Study in Scarlet** by Arthur Conan Doyle:

"I consider that a man's brain originally is like a little empty attic, and you have to stock it with such furniture as you choose. A fool takes in all the lumber of every sort that he comes across, so that the knowledge which might be useful to him gets crowded out, or at best is jumbled up with a lot of other things, so that he has a difficulty in laying his hands upon it.

Now the skillful workman is very careful indeed as to what he takes into his brain-attic. He will have nothing but the tools which may help him in doing his work, but of these he has a large assortment, and all in the most perfect order. It

is a mistake to think that that little room has elastic walls and can distend to any extent. Depend upon it there comes a time when for every addition of knowledge you forget something that you knew before. It is of the highest importance, therefore, not to have useless facts elbowing out the useful ones."

Most people only quote the first paragraph of this Sherlock Holmes statement (and some quote only the first sentence), but the second paragraph is of equal significance though perhaps not as colorful in imagery. The amazing thing to realize, however, is that in the more than 100 years since that appeared in **A Study in Scarlet**, science has proven it was largely correct in its conclusions about the function of memory, and how we take in, retain, and access memories.

The thrill of discovering this for me at the age of twelve impacted my life in some dramatic ways. Added to this was the description of Holmes considering as "useless facts" things like basic astronomy, literature, and philosophy. He has immense knowledge of the tools he needs to help him in his work, like his extensive studies into the many varieties of cigar ash.

How Sherlock Almost Cost Me My High School Diploma

I kept this in mind as I went to Lincoln High School in Philadelphia. As part of an experiment in education, Lincoln decided to let students in their junior year select their major subjects for study in the senior year. I was in my glory! I got to try out Sherlock Holme's theories. I did not take a single science or math class, but instead enrolled in five English majors, including College English, and English Literature, and since I never bothered to remember useless information, I couldn't tell you what the others were if my life depended upon it. As it turned out my graduation almost did depend on it.

It turned out that I was signed up for the academic curriculum designed for students who planned to go on to higher education. And for this, math and science classes were required. Since I was lacking in those subjects, the school, three months before graduation, threatened to not give me a diploma. My parents were called into the principal's office and they pointed out that the school itself had permitted me to avoid algebra, geometry, calculus, and biology. I saw no reason, with my aspiration to be a fiction writer, to take in any of this information. The school relented, and I graduated with an academic degree in the top fifth of my class. Mainly, I believe, because I loved taking tests, and thus rarely scored less than a 100 or A+, even though I also rarely did my homework assignments. I was warned that if I wanted to go on to college, I would probably have to make up my educational deficiencies. There is a very good book out, if you feel you would like more information about the Sherlock Holmes theories on all this, and how modern brain science has proven many of them to be true. I first started writing about the mind as an attic in the early 1990s, as I saw it as very relevant to the process of reprogramming our minds with positive information to offset all the negative stuff cluttering our attics. In just the past couple of years, several books have come out purporting to teach us how to think like Sherlock Holmes (I'd much rather learn how to think like his father, Arthur Conan Doyle). The best of these by far, and a book I recommend if you want to explore this further and scientifically, is **Mastermind:** *How to Think Like Sherlock Holmes* by Maria Konnikova. Konnikova writes for the New Yorker and blogs for Scientific American, graduated from Harvard, and has a doctorate in Psychology from Columbia. At Harvard, her mentor was bestselling author, Steven Pinker. She started her knowledge of Sherlock Holmes a lot earlier than I did, at the age of four when her father read her the stories in Russian. I found a quote by her that closely echoes something I have been talking about for many years, the importance of reading fiction as well as nonfiction. She said,

"I tell this to everyone ... I think you lead an impoverished life if you only read nonfiction ... I think the best psychologists are actually fiction writers. Their understanding of the human mind is so far beyond where we've been able to get with psychology as a science ... You need the careful experimentation, but you also need to take a step back and realize that fiction writers are seeing a broader vista and are capable of providing you with insights or even ideas for studies."

This certainly fits in with my own theory that novelists are the keenest observers of the human condition. And Arthur Conan Doyle was among the most keen. Just in the past couple of years I read some of his non-Sherlock novels, there's a whole slew of them, and his comments on human behavior, religion, philosophy, science, and medicine put him way ahead of his time of the late 19th Century and early 20th Century.

Konnikova says Sherlock Holmes had a great impact on her life and her educational choices.

Back to the mind as an attic, Maria Konnakova says this in **Mastermind**:

"To cultivate our knowledge actively, we need to realize that items are being pushed into our attic space at every opportunity. In our default state, we don't often pay attention to them unless some aspect draws our attention. But that doesn't mean they haven't found their way into our attic all the same. They sneak in if we're not careful, we just passively take in information and don't make a conscious effort to control our attention, especially if they are things that somehow pique our attention naturally. Topics of

general interest. Things that raise some emotion in us, or things that capture us by some aspect of novelty or not."

Dealing With Those Sneaky Thoughts

Especially nowadays, when the Internet adds exponentially to the mind clutter, we need to find ways to control the flow in. I describe what is going on with all the facts and non-facts being hurled at us twenty-four hours a day as Information Asphyxiation. Our creative mind is literally being choked by this deluge of useless information. What to do about it? Well, to take another lesson from Sherlock Holmes, to start with we have to become much better at editing what comes in with discernment and good selection skills. These can be developed to counter the default position most people have, who are as Maria Konnikova says, not careful and therefore allow information in passively instead of controlling our intake with conscious attention. Passive income is great, passive acceptance of swarms of useless information is not.

A New Immigration Policy

A new immigration policy for our brains is much more vital than one for our physical borders. We need to become more discerning border guards and gatekeepers. As I was pondering all this, I went off on a speculative tangent and began to wonder if Alzheimer's was impacted by overstuffed memories subjected to a long life of badly chosen attic furniture. It does seem to make sense that this might be so, in addition to any physical brain deterioration, which has been documented. But much of this research is only in its beginning stages. I think it would certainly be useful to do a study on how being more selective and more assertive in the information we let in affects our aging brains. An overstuffed attic can hardly be conducive to youthful brain agility and acuity.

Moneylove Action Exercise

I have had people say to me, *"Why do you call them action exercises when many involve just thinking about something, or answering questions for yourself?"* Anyone who doesn't think thinking is action, perhaps should read some books or take some classes on the brain, and how many functions are involved in thinking even simple thoughts. Luckily, we don't have to know how all this activity is going on, we can just enjoy the power it gives us to create, think, and remember.

For this exercise, I want you to take pen to paper or journal and make a list of: **10 Things I Know That I Don't Need to Know.** What will making this list accomplish? For one thing, it will make you more aware that you have indeed not been fully responsible or discerning in what you let in, so you will have to be more diligent and discriminating from now on. There are two issues, two parts of The Law of Subtraction. One is to set up that healthier new immigration policy. Be intentional as well as attentional.

Attentional?

Well, i didn't know it when it popped into my mind as a good accompaniment for "intentional". And thanks to Google, I have found myself a legitimate new word. It's defined as: directing the mind to an object; a concentration of the mind on a single object or thought; a capacity to maintain selective or sustained concentration; the ability or power to keep the mind on something. So it fits in very well with The Law of Subtraction in terms of what we take into our minds from the huge amount of information, mostly junk information, out in the world.

It also reinforces the idea that one way to edit what comes into our mind attic, as Maria Konnikova says, is by conscious effort to control our attention. This will take practice, but it is something that you can start immediately. One way was suggested by Lance Morrow, whose great quote opening this chapter is worth repeating, and thinking about, being attentional about:

The mind takes its shape from what it holds, and therefore, Zen-like, sometimes grows more graceful because of what it has kept out.

Before we get to the solution to some of the problems Lance Morrow came up with, it's time for another,

Moneylove Action Exercise

This exercise came to me inspired by something Martin Boroson says in the upcoming **TimeLove** section. Martin says that if we take a moment to meditate in the middle of busy activity, the mind grows more spacious. And it was also suggested by one of the 100 Quotercises I have in the Book Eleven **QuoteLove** segment, which takes a favorite quote and changes one or more words to see how that changes the quote for better or worse. I was looking at Lance Morrow's quote, which has become a favorite over the twenty-some years since I first read it in TIME magazine, and I think "spacious" might work as well or even better than "graceful." What do you think?

The mind takes its shape from what it holds, and therefore, Zen-like, sometimes grows more spacious because of what it has kept out.

Whether you like my change or not, the exercise I suggest you do is to take a few moments and actually think about how spacious your mind, or your mind attic is. When I did this, I pictured a couple being shown a large attic for rent by a real estate agent. It is relatively empty, and the woman says, "Wow, this is really spacious, let's take it." And then I visualize the alternative version, where the attic is stuffed with all kinds of junk, and the woman says, "What a cluttered mess, let's get out of here." It's the same attic in both scenarios, the difference being in what has been let in or stored there. So ask yourself this question:

"Is my mind attic stuffed to the ceiling with useless junk, or is it spacious so that there is room for valuable new thoughts and ideas to enter?

Brain clutter not only makes it more difficult to receive new worthwhile information, but may create a state of confusion when you try to retrieve something that is stored there and you want immediate access to.

What I find amazing is the current brain science is confirming a lot of what Sherlock Holmes/Arthur Conan Doyle said about 130 years ago, that,

"It is a mistake to think that that little room has elastic walls and can distend to any extent. Depend upon it there comes a time when for every addition of knowledge you forget something that you knew before."

Brain scientists are finding out that the brain storage system, our memory, may indeed be finite, almost like a physical building with limited space, like an attic in fact. Now the brain has huge storage capacity, but it apparently, as Holmes said, is not limitless, and this will, at some point, impact our capability to store new information or retrieve older memories.

What Lance Morrow suggested in his essay over twenty years ago (the date doesn't appear on the TIME page I saved, and I can't find any reference to the article at all, but I first quoted it in a piece I did about the mind-attic for a workshop workbook in 1991) is that we learn to recuse ourselves from useless information. In fact, the TIME essay is titled, Let Us Recuse Ourselves Awhile.

The word "recuse" is usually used in reference to judges removing themselves from cases in which they might have a conflict of interest. But Lance Morrow wrote:

"Perhaps this is an idea whose time has come. The intellectual attic is stuffed now. Urgent, exotic pieces of lumber are gathering in the mind from all over the world. They are tumbling out the windows."

But if was bad then, and it was as the 24/7 news cycle was already with us in 1991, imagine how much it has expanded now that we have the Internet. There is so much more need to be attentional and discerning now that there was in the late 19th Century when Sherlock Holmes first talked about his mind attic, or even in the late 20th Century. And still Lance Morrow wrote:

"We live in inundations of information. The air is dense with billions of fleeting names, images, factoids, electronic dust. But there is a way to impose order on this incoherence. The mind must be a discriminating host. It needs a bouncer at the door."

So whether you call it a bouncer or border guard, do realize that the person guarding your mental gates is you. Morrow also said:

"Creative recusal means that you refuse delivery on unwelcome items of knowledge. Recusal does not discourage curiosity. On the contrary, it allows curiosity to breathe and put down roots. It clears some of the junk out of the garden, pulls up a few weeds."

One way we can become a more effective bouncer or border guard for our mind attic is to start refusing to take delivery on some items from the popular culture. As I have stated, I have three criteria for spending my time or picking a project, or taking in stuff to my mind attic. That is to decide whether this is bringing me Knowledge, Pleasure, or Profit.

One of the habits I developed for myself and recommended to my students, coaching clients, and workshop participants is to have a moratorium on the news, which I guess can be called recusing yourself from the news. That's TV and radio and newspaper news reports. As a former newsman, I am well aware that it is all biased toward to violent and tragic, not very good messages or energy to allow in. Then there's all the cultural fluff we are exposed to and need to take precautions against.

Are you really getting any knowledge, pleasure, or profit from following the exploits of the Kardashians?

Moneylove Action Exercise

Make a list of ten people or topics you have allowed to passively enter your mind that you are willing to recuse yourself from, and never read about or look up information about again.

Next, ask yourself this question, and give an honest answer:

"Do I ever let trivial, unimportant, or useless information in as a way of avoiding doing what I need to do to move forward in my life?"

In other words, are you a mind attic hoarder, filling your memory with all sorts of junk you will never use? Or is your mind attic stocked with items by intention, by conscious choice, so that specific information you desire is easily accessible?

An overstuffed attic will certain limit your ability to make positive changes in your life and in your consciousness.

A Way to Deal With Unwanted and Unneeded Information

When I was involved in biofeedback alpha training as a Founding Director of The Biofeedback Institute in New York, I would guide students using brain wave biofeedback devices to learn how to produce alpha brain waves. As one of the main obstacles to achieving this meditative state are random thoughts and memories coming to the surface, I had a suggestion on how they could be successfully bypassed. I would have the student imagine they were floating on a river and whatever distracting thoughts would pop up could easily be neutralized by simply thinking, "Not now, please pass on by," and to picture those thoughts gently floating past.

You can do the same "pass on by" exercise when information or memories come out of your attic that you haven't requested. But with this "Pass on by," instruction, picture that you are banishing them from your memory banks entirely. Understand this, your mind if filled with a lot of useless junk furniture and it's time for a mental yard sale.

For the future, you need to realize that just because something attracts your attention doesn't mean you have to give it more than a momentary glance, there is usually no need to store it for future reference. If you haven't achieved all your dreams and aspirations, there is lots of really valuable information needing your attention, but you need to make room for it.

Moneylove Action Exercise

Try out the "Pass on by," instruction when you are fully awake and alert and you are hearing or seeing or reading something you really don't want to be stored in your memory or mind attic.

This can be fun. Maybe sit in front of your TV and watch a reality TV show and say "Not now, pass on by." Or go to an email from an annoyingly persistent online marketer and say "Not now, pass on by," and it might not be a bad accompaniment to this to unsubscribe that person from your mail. Or, if someone comes up to you and you just know they are going to waste your time with something that is not useful, pleasurable, or profitable, say silently to yourself, "Not now, pass on by." If you feel comfortable enough, or perhaps just mildly uncomfortable, you can try saying it out loud, but let's just do one step at a time.

If Sherlock Holmes thought this was important, being careful about what you let into your mind attic, 130 years ago, before radio, television, or computers--and Lance Morrow voiced the need for a bouncer at your mental doorway before the Internet--imagine how imperative, how vitally essential doing so now is for your mental health, for freeing up your creative source, for making your mind more spacious, and for being able to pursue your aspirations on your true path without being held back by useless piles of furniture.

Renovate and Refurbish Your Attic

Replacing that old furniture in your mind attic may be long overdue. One idea that works for me is to picture it being tossed into a large trash bin every time you let a good or valuable thought or piece of information in. As one of the suggestions I have offered on diluting the impact of that little negative voice inside your head is to drown it in a sea of positive voices, information, people, and activities--you might do the same with the old furniture. Visualizing it being forced out by the incoming good stuff. I actually picture a huge trash dumpster just outside the entrance, right there in my mind, and ready to accept any furniture I no longer want or need, so it can be hauled off forever.

Sure, this analogy is simplistic, and the way your memory works is a lot more complicated. But I have talked to many brain scientists over the years and the truth is that there isn't a lot agreement on how the memory actually works. We do know more than we did in Sherlock Holmes' time, and even in 1991 when Lance Morrow probably wrote his essay. But there is still great accord in the brain research community that there is a lot of territory yet to be explored.

Your Brain Operates the Same

Everyone's brain operates in pretty much the same way, and what mostly separates each of us from everyone else on the planet are our memories and the choices and decisions we have made based largely on what we have taken in from parents, teachers and the experiences of our lives. In other words, taking control of this intake process is the most essential part of changing our lives for the better. And if, by conscious effort, we can remove some of the mental rubble and detritus we haven't needed or used since storing it, so much easier the task of clearing the mind and filling the attic with high quality furniture.

Einstein to the Rescue Again

I don't know if he read Sherlock Holmes, but Albert Einstein certainly understood the importance of keeping the mind uncluttered with useless information. He famously said:

"There's no need to memorize anything you can look up."

Einstein was referring to a library when he made that statement, although I wouldn't be surprised to find out he suspected the arrival of the computer age even though he died in 1955. Now, of course it is so much easier to look up stuff. And as a visionary and genius, there's a good chance he knew what was coming, a time when each of us has access to more information, literally at our fingertips, good and bad, useful and not, worth our attention and not, than Alexander The Great had in his huge library. And we don't have to go anywhere, seek the help of a librarian, or spend hours checking the card files.

Your Mind's Annex

A lot of things that are sent to us by life or by the Internet do not need to be retained beyond the moment. There is no good reason to waste attic space holding onto them. What you let in needs to be done with discernment, discrimination, common sense, and responsibility. We are the gatekeepers of our mind attics, and vigilance is necessary, more today than ever before in history. But we also have more help today than ever before, in the form of our computers.

It's about deciding for yourself, not passively taking in ideas and memories you need not have in your own hard drive. Your computer can now act as an external hard drive for the storage of most of it. I consider my computer an annex to my mind, a place to store things that I don't want cluttering up my memory. And now, with external storage facilities like the Cloud, you needn't even fill up your hard drive to do this.

My Email Solution

I sometimes add something to my "Not now, pass on by" statement. The expanded version is, "Not now, pass on by, but I may get to you later." What works for me is to use my email online storage, which is pretty unlimited, to store files I create for things I don't need to attend to immediately. For instance, as someone who is passionate about the English language, a lot of material, quotes, videos, etc. about English and grammar, is sent to me. I don't need to see it now, but imagine I will someday have some leisurely time to enjoyably immerse myself in it.

That may or may not happen, but I compose an email addressed to myself, where I put the links to all this English stuff, and just don't send it. So I have a really big file labeled English and filed under my Drafts designation on my email. It's there if I ever want or need it, but it isn't cluttering up my mind or my computer. I also have files on Art, Creativity, Humor, Animals, People to Someday Interview, etc.

Moneylove Action Exercise

Ask yourself this basic question:

"What information do I actually need to take into my mind, so that I can bounce it around, ponder it, use it to spur creative thinking in certain areas, or give me a better sense of direction in my life, or, again, bring me pleasure, profit, or useful knowledge."

You may actually need to take this question into your mind to bounce it around and ponder it. It's time to set up some standards and put that border guard in place with a strong immigration policy that also leaves your mental border open for welcome and useful information to come in. You might picture a tough border guard just outside your attic, providing tighter security along with openness to valuable new ideas. And inside, an equally tough bouncer who will throw out the useless ideas that are no longer serving you.

Create your own internal button that allows you to shut the gates to your mind so that you do not take in the information screaming to be allowed in, until and if you are ready to give it some attention.

Emotional Amplitude

Emotion plays a big role in what we take into our minds, and what we leave out. Strong emotion can fuel our attentional efforts to remember and to retrieve memory. The more passionate your commitment to starting to focus on and control on the information you are taking in, or the information you would like to remove, the more effective your efforts will be. As an example of the power of emotions over the mind, I have always liked a poem by F. W. Bourdillon:

The night has a thousand eyes, And the day but one; Yet the light of the bright world dies With the dying sun.

The mind has a thousand eyes, And the heart but one; Yet the light of a whole life dies When love is done.

And couldn't we do a whole seminar on that!

A Zen Tale About The Law of Subtraction

A university professor went to visit a famous Zen master. While the master quietly served tea, the professor talked about Zen. The master poured the visitor's cup to the brim, and then kept pouring. The professor watched the overflowing cup until he could no longer restrain himself.

"It's overfull! No more will go in!" the professor blurted. "You are like this cup," the master replied, "How can I show you Zen unless you first empty your cup?"

The most prominent and useful furniture in our mind attic is that which we focused on passionately and intensely. This is useful to know when we want to take in new information and new valuable ideas. Many people want to take in more than one idea at a time, but it is important that we realize that we always have the option to put intense attention on one idea, on something we want to achieve or learn or manifest, and it will be more deeply embedded and more easily accessible than mind furniture we have carelessly flung into our attic.

Swami Vivekananda's Thoughts on Thought

Over a hundred years ago, the great Hindu spiritual master, Swami Vivekananda, talked a lot about how the brain works, and how it can be our great servant and asset, and how we can use it more effectively to achieve our goals and dreams.

In a statement that is as relevant today, maybe even more so, than it was back then, Swami Vivekananda referred to the brain and its capacity to focus in a single-minded way:

"Take up one idea. Make that one idea your life--think of it, dream of it, live on that idea. Let the brain, muscles, nerves, every part of your body, be full of that idea, and just leave every other idea alone. This is the way to success, that is way great spiritual giants are produced."

I've often stated that we all already know all we need to know to get everything we want...we just sometimes need to be reminded of that, need a stimulus to bring that knowledge up from the subconscious mind, to conscious awareness so we can put it into practice and action.

Swami Vivekananda said much the same thing:

"The goal of mankind is knowledge ... Now this knowledge is inherent in man. No knowledge comes from outside: it is all inside.

What we say a man 'knows', should, in strict psychological language, be what he 'discovers' or 'unveils'; what man 'learns' is really what he discovers by taking the cover off his own soul, which is a mine of infinite knowledge."

But the Swami Vivekananda quote I like the most, and the one most relevant in terms of the Law of Subtraction...comes from an era when most knowledge came from books...but it's as timely today in our age of the Internet as it was then:

"Books are infinite in number and time is short. The secret of knowledge is to take what is essential. Take that and try to live up to it."

What Is Essential

Of course, today, we could substitute facts or information or ideas for books in Swami Vivekananda's quote.

The secret of knowledge is to take what is essential no matter where that knowledge comes from, even from inside ourselves where most of it probably already exists.

To take what is essential. I remember so vividly hearing another late great mentor/teacher and friend, Leo Buscaglia, over thirty years ago giving a talk he called *What Is Essential Is Invisible To The Eye*. This is a phrase from

Antoine de Saint-Exupéry's **The Little Prince**. The full quote goes:

"And now here is my secret, a very simple secret; it is only with the heart that one can see rightly, what is essential is invisible to the eye."

We might consider how Saint-Exupéry's very humanistic way of thinking really paid off. **The Little Prince** has sold over 140 million copies worldwide since its initial publication in 1943. He wrote it while in exile in the U.S. after the Nazi invasion of France in World War II.

Moneylove Action Exercise

So, as our final exercise on The Law of Subtraction, let us focus on what is essential. Essential, meaning of utmost importance, indispensable, imperative. Here's your question and one you can repeat every time you are faced with new information clamoring to get inside your head:

"How much of what I take in or hold onto in my mind fits all the definitions of essential?"

Happy subtracting!

Book Four To Drown or Not Drown Stanley?

Who's Wavin'

I ain't wavin' babe, I'm drownin', Goin' down in a cold lonely sea. I ain't wavin' babe, I'm drownin'. So babe quit wavin' at me.

I ain't laughin' babe, I'm cryin'. I'm cryin', oh why can't you see? I ain't foolin' babe, I ain't foolin', So babe quite foolin' with me.

This ain't singin' babe, it's screamin'. I'm screamin' that I'm gonna drown. And you're smilin' babe, and you're wavin', Just like you don't hear a sound.

I ain't wavin' babe, I'm drowning'. Goin' down right here in front of you. And you're waving' babe, you keep wavin'. Hey babe, are you drownin' too?

Ric Masten

This book or segment is all about recognizing and eliminating much of your poverty consciousness. The obstacles holding you back from having what you want. But I want to explain the insertion of the Ric Masten poem that I first heard Ric deliver at the Miami Unitarian Church in the 1970s. Ric remained a friend until his sad passing in 2008 just before my release from Folsom. While I was in prison, we corresponded and he sent me all 23 of his books. My girlfriend and I visited he and his wife, Billie Barbara, in their mountaintop home at Big Sur once, and were very graciously entertained.

The reason I picked this poem out after I had thought I was pretty much done writing this book was something that

David Friedman, author of The Thought Exchange said to me. It was something very significant for me to hear, and it definitely proved that this old dog can learn some new tricks.

For many years, after writing **Moneylove**, I talked at workshops and on my audios about naming my inner pauper/negative voice, Stanley, and that the only way I (or anyone) could manage Stanley was to drown him in a sea of positive messages, images, and people, so that his power was diluted and diminished.

I still think this makes a lot of sense, and many people have reported to me in the past 25 years that this approach seemed to help remove negative energy in their lives. But now I have realized that there are other, just as valid, paths to moving past the Monkey Mind, Inner Pauper, and Stanley.

However, I will share some of the new ideas and information and take-home assignments that I've developed in the years since I invented Stanley.

Actually, all of Moneylove 3.0 is an antidote for the poison of poverty thinking, especially most of the exercises and experiential processes I suggest.

In my seminars, I talked about my inner pauper, that little negative voice that says, "You can't do it." "You don't deserve to have money easily come to you." "Your life isn't working and there's nothing you can do about it." That's Stanley, and he still shows up from time to time. An important point is that you never totally rid yourself of your Stanley. Every one of my extremely knowledgable contributors agrees with that basic premise. The negative messages instilled by your parents, significant others in your life, and the culture itself, are so deeply embedded that he is bound to pop up from time to time.

When it comes to losing Stanley, realize that like Waldo, he will always be there somewhere. But you can have him under strict surveillance and constraint.

Each of my 12 Books has information and exercises that will help you contain your version of Stanley.

A few of the games and exercises I suggest at the end of this book should do the job quite easily. But if your negative poverty voice is deeply embedded in your subconscious so that these exercises, or other methods such as affirmations and meditation, don't seem to give you a powerful enough solution, you might want to consult a professional. Though before doing that, finish this Book Four, and read carefully over what my fellow faculty members, collaborators and contributors, especially David Friedman, Dr. Marta Vago, Dr. Maria Nemeth, Rev Maggy Whitehouse, and Dr. Rickie Moore have to say, as they offer some powerful solutions to dealing with that pesky inner voice.

Frame of Reference

Quite recently, I've been exploring a tool psychologists and psychiatrists use when working with patients blocked in some specific area of their lives, such as money. Frame of reference, to me, means the way in which you view the world, the foundation from which most of your perceptions emerge. It is an important concept to understand and recognize, because we all have frames of reference for every aspect of our lives, and just knowing they exist can help in moving forward and upward.

One definition that is useful I found in the Fontana Dictionary of Modern Thought:

Frame of Reference: The context, viewpoint, or set of presuppositions or of evaluative criteria within which a person's perception and thinking seem always to occur, and which constrains selectively the course and outcome of these activities.

I also like one of the first statements on the subject, before it was even called "Frame of Reference," by the late dean of American columnists, Walter Lippman, who died in 1974 at the age of eighty-five. Lippman was a deep thinker, and he is credited with being the first to use the term, "cold war," as well as coining the term, "stereotype." His landmark book was **Public Opinion**, published in 1922. The following is from that book.

"We are told about the world before we see it. We imagine most things before we experience them. and those preconceptions, unless education has made us acutely aware, govern deeply the whole process of perception. They mark out certain objects as familiar or strange, emphasizing the difference, so that the slightly familiar is seen as very familiar and the somewhat strange as sharply alien ..."

Are you getting the idea of why Frame of Reference is such a big deal?

I think it might be useful to explore it further in terms of prosperity and poverty consciousness with my good friend, the brilliant therapist and business consultant, Dr. Marta Vago.

I interviewed Marta just as she and her husband, pianist Stephen Manes were about to embark on one of their many luxury cruises. I only mention that because I think that it illustrates that Marta knows how to create a life of passion, joy, and lots of fun.

The Wisdom of Marta Vago, PhD

I remember Eric Berne, the father of Transactional Analysis, saying, "There are two kinds of people, rich and poor, and it has little to do with how much money they have."

What he meant was that a person who believes they're rich, may not have a cent to their name, but the way they will explain that to themselves is *"Well, I'm a rich person but right now I'm having a little hard time, but that's just right now."*

A person who feels that they're poor, they could have millions of dollars in the bank and they will not have any psychological ownership of that wealth. They will say, "Oh yes, that's all very nice for now, but who knows when it's all going to go away."

It All Comes Down to This

It comes down to one's frame of reference. About money, wealth, financial well-being. A frame of reference acts like a filter in which we perceive, experience, interpret, and react to whatever isn't in our environment.

What do we notice? What do we ignore? What do we believe? What do we not believe? What do we perceive? And what do we turn into something else? Who or what are we attracted to, and who or what are we not attracted to? What kind of people or what kind of events seem to be magnets for us? How do we basically interpret what we think and feel from moment to moment?

Your Most Important Skill

So it is a filter and it is selective. Understanding one's frame of reference around money or wealth or anything else, to me, is the most important personal skill one could have. Because how you perceive and explain something to yourself determines what actions you're going to take, or what things you are not even going to notice. And there is a self-perpetuating quality to this frame of reference.

I've always said there is a certain miserable comfort in knowing what to expect, no matter how bad it is--at least you know what you're doing. It's no accident that some people marry two or three alcoholics in a row. There is a certain miserable comfort in knowing what to expect from a person, and in structuring one's interactions to make it happen. And most people don't like surprises--maybe a surprise party once in a blue moon--but most people like feeling that they have control.

So when it comes to understanding our relationship to money, and prosperity, and how to structure our time, I think it's critical to have an in-depth understanding of all the variables that make up our frame of reference. because that frame of reference, until or unless it is changed, is going to dictate how we move forward and what we can expect going forward.

The Big Three

According to Eric Berne, a frame of reference basically answers three questions, the answers to which account for recurring patterns throughout one's life: Who am I? What am I doing here? Who are all these others?

By age six, for better or worse, a person has a self-definition of who they are, what they're doing here on Earth, and who all the other people around them are. So, a lot of it is unconsciously locked in by the time they're six years old and will predispose them to certain choices and actions throughout life..

Now if they happen to be lucky and come from a family that basically has prosperity consciousness, then chances are excellent that they too have a prosperity consciousness going way back. However, not too many people are that fortunate. So through good counseling, or therapy, or coaching, they need to get a handle on all the aspects of their frame of reference including focusing on the whole notion of money and prosperity, and love and poverty and all that. So that they can paint a picture for themselves, fill in the blanks of 'What does my frame of reference consist of?' And to the extent that I believe in these things, what are the effects of that?

And with professional help, they can, one by one, reframe the aspects of that filter. So, I know that I'm inclined to read articles that have to do with losing money, poverty, what have you. I know that I'm inclined to do that--but being inclined is not a life sentence. You can make, for example, a conscious decision to change your reading habits. Or, I notice that I'm inclined to hang out with people who have money problems. Okay, that's an inclination and you don't have to give into it. With true volition, you began to search out and approach and reach out to people whose consciousness would be more healthy for you.

So, with time, and with a lot of discipline to monitor what you're doing and how you're doing it, you can reduce the influence of that very early programming.

Having said that, we all need to be vigilant that under extreme and crisis circumstances the human tendency is to revert back to whatever we learned and started to believe in before we were six years old.

We have to be extra vigilant when we are undergoing a lot of stress, or when things are going on around us that are likely to trigger parts of that old frame of reference. So we don't fall prey to them, so that we can remain in that learned or adopted frame of reference even though the little kid in us wants to slide back to what they felt and thought when they were five or six years old.

We need to be extra vigilant under those stressful or crisis situations because all the new awarenesses and beliefs can sometimes be overwhelmed by what's going on around you."

What Marta is basically saying is that, like your negative inner pauper,

a new, more positive frame of reference can also be drowned out by lots of

bad things happening, either to you or around you. Her own frame of

reference was influenced by a major event in her early life.

The Deeper Story

Let's go back to the 1956 Hungarian Revolution, which Marta and her family were in the midst of in Budapest. As she recently told me,

I remember when the Hungarian Revolution broke out in 1956. We had exactly two hours to figure out whether we were going to escape. My parents came to me and said, "It doesn't matter any more to us where we live and die. It's going to be your decision whether to leave Hungary and live elsewhere. And you have two hours to make up your mind, two hours until we have to take the clothes on our backs and get out the door."

I had all the reasons in the world, because of the horrors my parents went through during the Holocaust and everything, I had every reason in the world to just collapse and roll over and play dead. But somehow during all the awful circumstances during their lives, they managed to instill in me a sense that there was something better out there. And because I have that, thanks to them, I was able to say to them in an hour or hour-and-a-half, "Let's leave."

And I supposedly had everything going for me in Budapest. I was studying with the best piano teacher in the country, and if my parents, despite their horrible experiences during the war and after, hadn't instilled in me a belief that there was a better way, I'm not sure if I would have been able to come up with that decision to leave.

And I don't know to this day. I don't know, because of the stress of that last month in Hungary during the revolution, hand grenades going off, and people getting hung from trees right outside our house, and living in the basement.

I think my musical education helped, too, as it's about timing, and following through, and bettering yourself. It's about playing better tomorrow than you did today. It's preparing for the next concert and you have the responsibility to do the best you can. I think all of those things together allowed me to make what turned out to be a very prudent choice.

A Quote About Changing Your Frame of Reference

It so happens that one of my very favorite quotes, which I had drawn in calligraphy thirty years ago, so I could put it on my wall and have its powerful message constantly reinforced, really is about the steps to changing your frame of reference. It's from Thomas Huxley, English scientist of note in the 19th Century:

Sit down before fact as a little child, be prepared to give up every preconceived notion, follow humbly wherever nature leads, or you will learn nothing.

And now some exercises and strategies to help you change or gain some insight into your frame of reference concerning money and prosperity and poverty.

Moneylove Action Exercise

This first was one of the first tools I developed to help people become aware of all the negative stuff we allow into our minds, and some of the negative things we may be saying to others. Since she was kind enough to put it in her multimillion copy bestseller, You Can Heal Your Life, I'll defer to the words of Louise Hay on this, as she gives a great short description:

Jerry Gillies, who has written MONEYLOVE, one of the best books I know on money, suggests we create a Poverty Penalty for ourselves. Every time we think or say a negative about our money situation, we fine ourselves a certain amount and put it in a container. At the end of the week, we have to spend this money on pleasure."

I really haven't much to add to what Louise said in her book, other than it should be an amount you can afford, but preferably one that will cost some discomfort as you place it in your poverty penalty box, or whatever other container you want to use. It will build up faster than you will expect, so you can start thinking about what kind of pleasure reward you will get for yourself once it reaches a certain amount.

Moneylove Action Exercise The Compliment Bulletin Board

I created this strategy several years after writing **Moneylove**, when I realized the potent effect of the compliments other people pay me. Not only do they feel good, but they really affect my prosperity consciousness. The idea, as I originally conceived it, was that every time someone paid me a compliment that felt good, I'd ask them to put it in writing and sign it. No one ever refused me, as it was also a compliment to them for me to say theirs was special for me. Now, I often get those compliments by email, and so I now have a virtual Compliment Bulletin Board, as well as an actual one.

Often we have a momentary burst of pleasure or pride when someone pays us a compliment, and then let go of it, or let it fade away.

I think it's important to recognize that these positive praise statements offered to you are fantastic natural resources you can use to bolster your spirits and raise your appreciation of who you are as a person.

I first related the story of one compliment that had special meaning for me on my Moneylove album by Nightingale-Conant. A counselor friend of mine was working with actress Linda Gray, who is one of the most spiritual and prosperity conscious people in show business. She was then making over $60,000 each week playing Sue Ellen Ewing on Dallas. My friend gave her a set of my Seminar-In-A-Package cards. 20 Affirmative messages. She sent me a note saying simply:

"You have made a positive dent in my life."

I got a picture of Linda and put it and the compliment up on my board. I also have Louise Hay's nice comment on Moneylove, and just looking at it reminds me of many fond memories from our friendship, which started before she believed she could be prosperous. In fact, this multimillionaire healing and self-help icon, was having trouble turning her small healing booklet into a full-sized book. Now she owns her own super successful Hay House publishing empire.

Moneylove Action Exercise

There's an exercise participants in my prosperity workshops really seemed to get value out of, in terms of recognizing some of the negative messages they may have gotten from their parents, messages that helped form their frame of reference as adults.

I would have the group break into A and B designated players. To start off, I would tell the A people that they were going to play the child they were, perhaps at the age of 8 or 9. I asked them to go around and ask the B people for money, as they asked their own parents as a child. The B players were to portray one of their parents, giving the A people the kind of answers they themselves got when asking for money as a child. Then we switched roles. What came up for a lot of the people doing the asking was how they may have started out asking boldly for what they wanted, but then became increasingly timid as many of their requests for money were turned down.

During their role as one of their own parents, they were surprised at how quickly they remembered some time-honored phrases, such as:

"Do you think I'm made of money?" "I work hard to put a roof over your head and food on the table." "Money doesn't grow on trees."

The participants in this game also realized that negative attitudes from their parents were dictating some of their current attitudes about money and success. They particularly remembered changing from directly asking for money to feeling they had to come up with some "good" or "sensible" purpose for the money they were requesting, and therefore learned to lie at an early age.

Of course, some people had parents who were prosperity conscious, though few of those emerged during the interactions. Their response to requests for money might include:

"Sure, are you certain that's all you need?" "You don't have to tell me what it's for, how much do you want? "You know all you have to do is ask."

Any of those remind you of your childhood?

You can just think about those early days and how your parents taught you directly and indirectly about the position of money in one's life. Of course, they were operating from what may have been a negative frame of reference passed down through generations.

But I would suggest it will be a much more valuable experience if you choose a partner to play with, a close friend or loved one. Take turns being the parent and the child and see what useful information comes up.

Looking at Your Poverty Programming

Now it's time to look at some of this early negative programming that holds us back. comedian and minister and author of the **Prosperity Teachings of the Bible Made Easy**, Maggy Whitehouse, says:

Sometimes people dive into positive thinking and prosperity thinking a little too swiftly; it really takes baby steps because it's important to get yourself to accept a little more happiness every week rather than trying to go for the whole hog at once. The ego won't accept such a big shift and, if you don't go slowly, it will often hit back. Just look at lottery winners who lose all the money

in a short time and end up unhappier than before or people who get a windfall and then find it's all eaten up by a problem with their house or their health.

It's also important to look at what your concept of God may be. There is often this childhood thing sitting inside us making us think there's a judgmental old man in the sky who's going to punish us if we don't do enough voluntary work or enough 'good things' or if we don't give our money away. A lot of my work over the years has been about helping people bring up and resolve this underlying belief that God is going to punish them for something --especially for daring to be rich. The ego will work that angle all the time and it causes terrible distress.

Jesus Was Not Poor

We're all taught, for example, that Jesus was poor (consequently 'good' people should be poor). So what happened to the gold, frankincense and myrrh that his family were given by the three Magi? How come Joseph was a mason? (usually translated as carpenter) — a builder, in fact — which was an excellent trade in those times especially in a town like Nazareth which was only four miles from the metropolitan centre of Sepphoris which was being rebuilt when Jesus was a child.

But more importantly than this, Jesus was a teacher who could manifest whatever he needed whenever he wanted it. He didn't go in for clutter and he warned against our being possessed by possessions--but he could trust that all he needed would be there in perfect time. That's real prosperity and the Bible is full of teachings on how we can all achieve that, whatever the spoilsports may like to imply!

www.MaggyWhitehouse.com

As you can see, for me one of the great things about including several very gifted prosperity thinkers and teachers in the mix of this book is that one can often see where their thinking on some facets of working toward a more fulfilling level of prosperity consciousness starts out with similar ideas, but then they each do something slightly different with the basic premise that we all have some deep-rooted fears and limitations about money and success. Marta Vago, for instance, focuses on our frames of reference, while Maggy Whitehouse talks about this childhood thing that sits within each of us. Getting a bit more complex (at least that's my belief because I often have to ponder his concepts longer than others), is David Friedman. It's not that his approach isn't a simple one, but that it simply asks us to see it all in a new way, and come up with a specific, unique solution.

David Friedman and the Thought Exchange Process

David is a well known composer, who also conducted the orchestra for a number of Disney animated films. He is also a producer, having most notably worked closely with the late Nancy Lamott, including writing her signature song, Help is On the Way. David has acted as a coach for professional singers and actors and often gotten them to new levels of performance using a technique he calls, **Thought Exchange**, which is the title of his book on this subject. He has now moved into working with non-performers, executives and entrepreneurs. David Friedman is one of the teachers and mentors I have learned a lot from. I may not always grasp what he is trying to teach me right away, but it works anyway. I love his subtitle for the book, *Overcoming Our Resistance to Living a Sensational Life.* That's what it really is all about, and most of my prosperity teaching friends and contributors agree that prosperity is a natural event, out there for all of us to enjoy, and the only thing that prevents this is our individual resistance to having it all, or as David puts it, Living a Sensational Life!

Because it can seem difficult to go deeply into our physical sensations and identify them and the thoughts we have connected with them, I felt I wanted to give David a lot of space to explain it all. He also has been working on a new book about the power of negative thoughts and uncomfortable sensations, so I first asked him about that natural follow-up to **The Thought Exchange**. I also told him how much I loved and how much value I got out of listening to his song, Help is On The Way, so much so that I use its lyrics to open Book Seven, **Building A Prosperous Spirit**. I told him that my other favorite song that I felt was like a seminar all by itself was the great 1943 classic, Accentuate the Positive. David started with:

I absolutely love accentuating the positive, but one of the things that happens is that people think they're going to feel comfortable when they're successful and they think that you should get rid of negative thoughts, that's the little child coming to you and saying, "I'm upset," and you saying, "Cancel, cancel, I banish you and you're out of here!" You can't do that because that is your history and you have to own that and hear that and feel that.

One of the things I deal with a lot is that when people actually get what they want, they are very much in pain and very much in anxiety because it was dangerous to get what they want previously. And unless people can allow themselves to feel as uncomfortable as they feel when they're successful, they won't let themselves be successful.

I often say to people who say they want to be successful, "Are you willing to be that uncomfortable?" For instance I say, "Are you willing to be someone who is criticized all the time, your decisions affect many many people's lives, and people are constantly upset about those decisions, and whose job depends completely on what people think of you?" If not, you're not willing to be President of the United States. Or, "Are you willing to be someone who had a really impoverished, abusive upbringing, who now is very powerful, but everyone wants something from you all the time, and everyone is constantly scrutinizing you about who you're with, what you do, how much you weigh?" If you can't do that, you can't be Oprah Winfrey. So, people admire these people, and they don't realize what a challenge it is to be these people.

People have this illusion that they're going to feel good--there was one new thought saying I saw that said, "You know you're on the right track when you feel good." Baloney! I just had some successes recently, and I am so anxious and so uncomfortable. These are things I hadn't allowed myself to have up to now, and now I know why.

A friend of mine said to me, "I don't know why I drink so much." So I said, "Would you like to find out why you drink so much?" And he said, "I really would." So I said, "Stop drinking and you'll immediately find out."

I think that one of the things that stops people is they're looking for the next book or the next method or the next whatever that will just let them circumvent everything and then they'll be fabulous and it'll be fine. But you do not circumvent yourself and things that happen in the world don't bypass that. It's like your little child is being left behind and it won't tolerate it.

I jumped in here to say, "It's like a beautiful mansion that sits on shaky ground that once was the site of a former toxic waste dump. You might get away with it for twenty years, but it's going to seep out sooner or later."

David responded:

Exactly! That's right! And it has to. And the thing about it is these things aren't bad, they're the little child in you. It's like a holiday when you go home to be with your family and your mother says that thing that drives you nuts. Be there with your inner child, and turn to your inner child and go, "Oh my God, you were right. You went through that, you went through that your whole life, how challenging for you." The thing is, you can tolerate your mother now. These things have to be mined and brought to the present.

And most of us live our lives trying to overcome this child, trying to crush it, trying to make it disappear, by being successful, by having money--it doesn't   work.

You have to go back and get the child. And then your natural ability, that's the thing that people don't recognize, that money and success and stuff is natural. Not some big weird thing that is being withheld from us. The use of our talents is natural to us. It's what comes up from the past that prevents us from doing that.

Thought Exchange came about because I noticed I was doing every metaphysical thing and I was not feeling good. I wasn't able to do it. They'd say, "Think positively," and I would think positively for two minutes and then I couldn't, and I thought, "I'm not stupid, I'm really interested in trying, what's going on here?" And I realized I was missing a whole piece of myself. In the same way as my upbringing, as most upbringings do, squelched it and couldn't tolerate it, I was actually doing that to myself. So I had to say, "Stop and look at, and allow to speak, those parts of you that are afraid.." And not just positivize over stuff that's there. You can't steamroller over it, you have to stop for it. So that you're a whole person when you're wealthy and successful, you're not covering something that's going to pop out.

It's what you see in the world that is what the world gives to you. The horrifying thing is I can go through life thinking I'm unhappy because I don't have enough money. Should I allow myself to get enough money, I may be happy about that for a moment, but then I notice to my horror that I'm unhappy because I'm unhappy. And that there is nothing that happens in the world that can change that.

That's why we really keep creating problems. The only place a problem exists is in your mind. If I have a financial problem right now, I'm just sitting here, there's nothing. I'm thinking about it. We create problems to get away from sensations. If we had no problems whatsoever, all we would have is our interior experience., we'd have our inner child. We keep ourselves in problems so that we don't have to find out that it's just an experience inside of us that we're afraid of.

We're running from something, and we have to turn around and face the dragon, and it is real! It's really hard to sit there and know I just feel empty because I feel empty, because there's a child I have in me that feels empty that never had anyone to feel empty with. And my job is to sit there with my inside and go, "Oh yes, I see how empty you feel, I see how upset you feel, I get it." No one else is going to get it in the same way. They can't, it's too late. It sort of sounds futile, because , "My God, no amount of money is going to make me happy?" But once you get this, the point is you can be happy with any amount of money. And you have the amount of money naturally that suits you. Life takes place only in our experience.

So, following along the path suggested by Dr. Marta Vago and Rev
Maggy Whitehouse, I asked David whether he agreed that the thoughts we
have, particularly the ones about early sensations that hurt us, are often
ones we're not aware of--because they are buried deep down within our
subconscious. He said:

Oh absolutely! If a sensation was connected with something painful, our whole psyche is about dancing away from that. Sometimes we create a thought about it, sometimes we don't even know we're thinking about it. Often when I start working with people, they don't even know they have sensations.

People will sometimes say, "I don't know, it's unconscious." And I say, "You want to know what it is? It's sitting right in front of you." That's the beauty, your unconscious is appearing in the world in front of you as a reflection. So you will often think, "Oh no, no, I'm being very positive." Look at what's going on in the world in front of you.

It has nothing to do with anything except your consciousness. It has nothing to do with what's objectively out there. So people will say, "No, no, I'm putting positive affirmations out there and I'm saying it's wonderful and I'm saying it's fabulous, and yet the money isn't coming." What thought are you having? And the thought is, "I can't have things, I always get stopped." You are seeing that thought. You cannot fight through that thought by getting more money. You have to see it and hear it and know that you have it. And allow it to speak. And allow yourself to feel the sensations that you took on that thought to avoid.

Strangely enough, positive thoughts cause the discomfort. We take on the negative thoughts to try to get away from discomfort. So you have the thought, "I can't get any money," because when you try to get money, it's painful. When you allow yourself to feel those sensations, then you will be able to deal with sensations that come with getting money. Not that you'll comfortable when you get money, but you'll be able to have money because you'll be able to be with what it feels   like when you have money.

As I listened carefully to what David had to say, which I always find enlightening as well as necessary, I had a thought which I expressed to him. I said it was the kind of a question I would ask if I were coaching him and he revealed how many of his own negative thoughts he had moved past. My thought was that in addition to confronting his sensations and the thoughts he created because of them, an additional reason for his success in dealing with these obstacles might be that this coincided with his beginning to coach and teach others what he was learning himself. I also told him about a great quote from our mutual friend, Sonya Milton. She was the minister at Unity San Francisco when he did a very brilliant workshop and also a fantastic concert of his music there. Sonya says, *"I teach to understand what I'm thinking."* And to that quote, David responded:

That's right. I always say when I do these challenging workshops, I say to my students, "I am not sitting here on the mountaintop teaching, I am going as crazy as you are, because I'm going through all of my own stuff while you're going through yours.

So while it sounds like his method requires a lot of work, and it can certainly be that for a lot of people with major issues about money or other things, I asked him if there is some simple, juicy tip he could share about dealing with negative thoughts and sensations.

The thing that I would say is that when you are confused, when you are in doubt, when you see something you don't know how to handle--stop and go to your sensations, and just experience them. Just go to your body, experience the tightness, the shakiness, the emptiness, whatever--don't analyze it. Of course you will analyze it. But as much as you can, just experience it. Get back to your experience and be with it.

That is very challenging, but you will find that it will bring you back to memories, it will bring you back to noticing where your mind goes when you dare to be in your body. It's amazing, we walk around in these bodies but we're terrified of experiencing them, terrified. So, I would say, when in doubt, when you have a problem and you don't know what to do, when you feel frightened, when things aren't working. Stop, go to your sensations and simply sit with them. It's like picking up a child and just holding it and

92

saying, "Tell me, tell me." Don't try to sooth them, don't try to calm them, don't try to release them. And that is really hard sometimes. Even for me, Mr. Thought Exchange.

During our conversation there came to me the Aha! moment when I decided to change the title of this segment from Drowning Stanley, so as to not be saying my long-held belief that the best way to deal with that negative poverty conscious voice was to inundate it with a sea of positivity, was the only solution. I didn't want to give the false impression, that I thought it was the only solution. even though it worked for me, especially during my twelve years in prison. My decision to make the change really happened when David said about my Stanley concept and similar ones:

A lot of people talk about letting it go, releasing it, relaxing it. I say, "No." I say, "Have it.""Live with it." If you're sitting there feeling very sad, and I'm giving you positive images, before I can give you positive images, I have to experience your sadness. I sing my song, Help Is On The Way, because I know there's help on the way, even though you don't. You have to get how upset Stanley is. You have to get that Stanley has a darned good reason for being upset. He's not stupid, he's not mistaken. Only when you can look and go, "Oh my, oh, oh I see, oh I see," then you can gently take him by the hand and you, the adult you, knows the truth that there's unlimited possibility.

But that child, Stanley, has never been heard. When I'm feeling upset, I don't want someone to tell me, "It's okay, you know, it's fine, you don't understand." It's saying, "Oh I hear how upset you are." I can hear it and not fall apart, I can hear it and not run away. I can hear it. That's what teaches the child that it's okay. That's what a good parent would have done.

If you try to drown Stanley, you're going to drown him, except he's not going to die. He's just going to be there screaming, "I'm drowning!" So try hearing Stanley first. Try going, "I get it." Stanley is making up those negative thoughts because he's afraid. Go to your sensations and find out what he's afraid of. You need to be very gentle with that inner child. Children do not need to be fixed, they need to be seen and heard. When we can do that, and it can be very hard, we start to grow into the present.

So as I digested all this, I said to David that many people might resist
doing the hard work, of having to feel uncomfortable, and they might need
more professional help and guidance to get in touch with their sensations
and thoughts. This might involve some of the people David is training to teach The
Thought Exchange concept, or even private coaching with David himself, or
possibly even a good therapist, as Marta Vago suggested might be
necessary to work effectively on one's Frame of Reference.
He responded,

Yes, you would need to then do something with a professional. But just to start with, I make the suggestion to people that they feel their sensations. Just as much as they can, go to their sensations., just to see if they can do that.

Start with that and see how you do. And notice if you jump away from those sensations, notice if you think they're terrible, and notice if you're attacking yourself, and notice if you think your sensations are going to kill you or are a danger to you. But just go to them.

The Thought Exchange began like a lot of other metaphysical processes and metaphysical systems and followed the idea that has often been expressed that your thoughts appear as a reflection of the world, and what you're thinking is mirrored in the world, I began to notice that even though everybody gets this, people don't seem to be able to do it. They take on a positive thought and then in five minutes they're not doing it, or they hit some obstacles and they drop it. So i began to explore why this happens.

An Invisible Experience

Donald Trump got rich using a certain method, but I say it's not his method that got him rich, but that he's holding a certain thought that other people who may apply his method are not holding. So I began to look for the seeds of what is in the way. What happens when you take on any thought is that you experience a sensation in your body. A sensation is not a feeling. A sensation is an experience. It might be tightness in your throat, a churning stomach, rushing blood. A sensation is just an invisible experience.

Learning From Your Sensations

So if you experience a sensation and that sensation is associated with some trauma or challenge in earlier life, for instance if, as a child you said "I can do this," and someone slapped you across the face, and said,"No you can't."

Every time now that you say or think, "I can do this," it will generate a sensation that you will interpret unconsciously as, "I'm going to get slapped across the face." And you will run from that sensation. Now, the only way we can run from a sensation, since sensations are generated by thoughts, is to take on a thought that won't generate that sensation. And that thought is what I call a "protective thought." We are not sabotaging ourselves, we are protecting ourselves.

We're smart people, we're committed people, we're spiritual people. We're not stupid, we're not just not doing it right. There's something we're protecting ourselves from. So, we will take on a thought to protect ourselves from the sensation that arises when we say, "I can do it." That thought will be, "I can't do it."

We live in these protective thoughts. And these protective thoughts produce results that we don't desire to see. The trouble is that while you do protect yourself from these sensations, as soon as you see results you don't want, you remember what it was that you did want and you're right back at the sensation.

So the only way we can apply the positive thinking and action we know will work, is to first be willing to experience the sensation we experience when we take on the thought of what we want. And that sensation is often uncomfortable. It's a ridiculous notion to think you are going to feel calm and comfortable when you begin to get what you want. Especially if it's something you've had trouble getting, you're going to feel completely uncomfortable.

It's not that you get a million dollars by having the thought, "I'm going to have a million dollars," and you made that happen. Because there's nothing to _make_ happen. I don't call it the Law of Attraction, because there's nothing to attract--everything is already here. I've always liked the way Buckminster Fuller described it. He said the world is a cube and everything's happening at the same time, but you're riding up an elevator in that cube, so you see this, and you see that, and then you see this, but _everything_ is happening.

The point is you're not making anything happen, but if the world is a mirror, you are seeing your thoughts in that mirror in any incident. My favorite example of this is when I was at a dinner party a few years ago. A woman was really in the middle of a messy divorce, and she was hating her husband. And she was saying, "That creep left me destitute! I don't know how I'm going to survive. He took everything except the apartment and I have to sell the apartment to survive. I don't know what I'm going to do!"

So someone asked, "What are you asking for the apartment?" And she said, "$7,750,000" We laugh at that because, poor thing, she's down to seven million dollars. But, in fact, imagine the destitution that you would have to experience <u>inside </u>in order to perceive seven million dollars as "destitute."

So if we are holding the thought of destitution, one of two things will happen. We will either see seven million dollars and think we're destitute, or we would spend our whole lives thinking, "If only I had seven million dollars, I wouldn't be destitute." But because, we are thinking, "I'm destitute," we will never see the seven million dollars that is all over the world, that is possible to see. When we understand that if we think that the physical world is real, nothing in spirituality makes sense at all.

When I say, "I am whole and well," and someone says, "No, you're not, you have the flu," they're right if the physical world is real. But inside in the infinite world of possibilities, I might have a raging fever, but be fine because peace is simply being able to be with what is, knowing that you already have everything in the only place you ever could have everything, which is on the inside.

We get all mixed up. We think that the object is to have things, to manifest. The purpose of manifesting is the same as the mirror. I get up in the morning and I look in the mirror, and I see the manifestation which is my image in the mirror. There's not a person in the mirror, there's the manifestation reflection of me. I might go, "Oh God, my hair's a mess." I don't go fix the mirror, I fix my hair. I use the mirror to see what it is I am looking like or thinking or whatever. That's the purpose of every trauma, of every upset. There's nothing going on there. There's nothing threatening or real. If I look at you and say, "You have a smudge on your nose," you wouldn't say, "How dare you tell me that!" You'd say, "Thank you," and wipe it off. And that's why we can have gratitude for every single thing that happens.

I always say, "Come to my seminars, you'll find out there's nothing to get, there's nothing to manifest, and you're going to feel lousy-wanna come?" That's what I have to offer. But really, what I have to offer is that you'll know that you have everything.

The Thought Exchange Seminar

Have you discovered the secret yet? No, not that **The Secret.** The secret I'm talking about is that you have been experiencing not just a few comments from David Friedman, but an entire seminar. I don't think this was our intention when we had our conversation, but like the best teachers, you just wind David up and let him go. A regular metaphysical Energizer Bunny.

Just to conclude this segment, this seminar, this whatever, I want to let you know something.

Why I Love the Way David's Mind Works

One of the reasons I love the way David Friedman's mind works is that he gives you so much substance to take into your mind and chew on. I personally think his concepts are graduate school to **The Secret's** kindergarten in terms of teaching us how to have what we want. I think his ideas teach us most of what we need to know about having prosperity, success, and creative fulfillment in our lives. It just makes so much sense to me, how about you?

A big part of my belief in what David is teaching is from having seen his techniques in action in a workshop he held in San Francisco. It was called, *Finding Your Inner Voice*, and was primarily aimed at professional singers, though a few of us who wanted to see him work attended, even me who cannot carry a tune (I know, that's a just a thought I have that can be exchanged). I saw him do amazing things. In brief ten or fifteen minute sessions, he coached singers to go beyond their fears and limitations to places they had never been before in terms of their singing performance.

Some of these singers were professional, some amateur, and in each individual coaching session, he had them exchange the thoughts that were limiting their singing performance, and they became better singers right before our eyes. One very good and pretty successful professional singer, I'll call Miss J, had the thought she couldn't hit a very high note in a specific song she wanted to perform. She had the sensation of tightening up all over, but especially in her throat, and the fear that she might damage her voice if she went for it. David worked with her for a few minutes and asked her to think she could hit that note with no discomfort.

Now here's a very important part of that, he told her she didn't have to believe she could hit the high note, she just had to focus on the thought that she could do it. You probably can guess that her rendition of that song was perfect, high note and all, and got a standing ovation. There's an awful lot of stuff out there on manifestation and the Law of Attraction. But it is one thing to hear or read theory, and quite another to see it in action.

www.TheThoughtExchange.com

99

A Wow Experience

Listening to David I thought about the power of our minds, and the necessity to sometimes go back in time in our memories, I suddenly remembered a profound experience I witnessed in Jamaica. during a workshop conducted by another great teacher, the legendary body therapist, Ilana Rubenfeld. We were outside on the beach and a massage table had been set up. One of the workshop participants had had a painful neck injury in a car accident a few years earlier, and had sought help from everyone, from chiropractors, psychic healers, orthopedic surgeons--no relief. And after several years of trying everything, she had almost given up.

Ilana hardly touched her, but had her relive the car crash and remember whether she had tightened up or loosened her muscles at the moment of impact. As you'd expect, she had tightened up. So Ilana asked her to visualize the moment of impact again, but this time imagine that she had stretched out her neck as far as she could, keeping it loose and flexible and making it as long as possible.

Even being right there on the beach seeing this, it was hard for any of us to believe that in an instant the pain and immobility in that woman's neck were gone! Gone for good, because I checked a few times over the following years with a mutual friend we had, and she had never had another episode of pain in her neck, and went on with her life as if the accident had never happened.

This story has not been told before, and neither has the next one. I think both are significant examples of how connected our thoughts and memories and bodies are. Coincidently enough (or should I say serendipitously enough?), my best friend, Rupa Cousins, worked closely with Ilana Rubenfeld, in her early days as an Alexander teacher, a highly respected form of body therapy. Ilana is perhaps the most honored and effective body therapist in the whole humanistic psychology and human potential field. She personally worked with Fritz Perls, the creator of Gestalt Therapy, where she developed the connections between emotions and the body.

Some years later Rupa became certified as a Rubenfeld Synergy Method practitioner, so is very well aware of this mind/body connection, and loves David Friedman's focusing on this aspect of dealing with our negative internal voice. In addition, Rupa is a relative of the founding father of psychoneuroimmunology, Norman Cousins, who led the way with his classic book, **Anatomy of An Illness**. Rupa is co-founder with Dr. Michael Gigante of the Northeast PNI Institute for Healing. For a definition of PNI or psychoneuroimmunology, I offer you the mission statement of The Norman Cousins Center for Psychoneuroimmunology at UCLA which "Investigates the interactions between the brain and the body, the role of psychological well-being for health and recovery from illness, and the translation of such knowledge into effective behavioral strategies that prevent disease, promote healing and enhance well-being across the life span." So much for the credentials that explain her devotion to the concept that the body knows all, and is very connected to our thoughts and emotions and spiritual energy. Now to her story.

Rupa's Tale

Rupa had always thought of herself as someone struggling about money. The reason goes back to her childhood and her mother, Sydne Cousins. Sydne was a very controlling mother and person. I knew her well from the time Rupa and I started dating. Sydne was also quite charming and a very successful businesswoman, first as a major buyer, and then as a designer, eventually creating her own lucrative business. Before she took her spiritual name, Rupa was Bonnie, and her mother invented a fastener she dubbed The Bonnie Clasp. It was the very first closure that allowed bras to be fastened and unfastened from the front. It was later adopted by the

U.S. Navy for its Mae West lifejackets. But Sydne always kept a tight hold on the purse strings. Rupa's father was out of the picture most of her life, so she was raised by a single parent who was somewhat of a workaholic.

Rupa tells, for the first time, the dramatic decision she made to change the early programming she got from her mom as a child. She says,

I had read that there was a way to change the past to create a new future, and one day I found myself traveling back in time with my imagination, to get to the source experience that had led me to always believe myself on the edge of poverty. The steps I needed to take to get to this "story" were to relax deeply, let go of any tension in my body, to go deeper into my inner self. This necessitated breathing, slowing down and finding a feeling of compassion in my heart so I could ask my little-girl-self to tell her story. I felt as if I was directly led to the memory of my four-year-old self, forced to go to nursery school by my mother, quite against my will. I could see my mother sending me off as she needed to get to work.

Then, I actually heard the conversation from back then as clearly as if it was happening in the present moment. My mother is telling me that she must work though she hates it. That she would much rather be with me. I think I knew even then that this was a lie, she loved her work, which probably had the positive effect of me eventually choosing work I loved to do.

But here's where the negative part comes in, my mother told me over and over again that she was the only one who would support me and that I would never have to worry that there would not be enough because, "I will always take

care of you." This became an unconscious thought and then a belief. Over and over again the same refrain played in my young mind, that she didn't like to work, that she would always take care of me, and that I wouldn't need to take care of myself. I got the very strong message that Mom would always take care of me, and I didn't have to, and that she was sacrificing herself for me. She wasn't doing it with any malice, but all the way into my young adulthood, she would need to come to my rescue because I couldn't take care of myself.

I grew up sort of helpless, her little doll. First as a mostly unemployed actor, then never making enough doing whatever work I did. When I went back to that four-year-old, I was watching her being fed a message that I had taken deep into myself, my inner self: That I would always need my mother to take care of me and that work was a hardship not to be enjoyed. In that moment I saw two lies that changed my life.

The lies were that I could never take care of myself, and that work was an unpleasant duty. The truth was that she actually loved her work and she loved the abundance it gave her, and I COULD take care of myself and enjoy it! And so, while I was in that deep heart space, I imagined my mother telling me that she loved me and her work, and that making money let us have a beautiful life and one day I would be able to do that too. It was a healing dialogue that brought me to tears. The new message melted the old one.

Almost magically as soon as I did this inner work, a call came from Ilana.

She was impressed with my work as an Alexander teacher and asked me to join her on a graduate course in the Alexander Technique for some of her Rubenfeld students. The one year course in New York turned into a two year course, and I was paid for individual sessions I gave to the students, so my income grew and grew. In fact, it increased threefold!

This lesson, it can be called in psychological terms, a "Reframe," continued to free my imagination and has continued to this day. Of course, what I did was change the tensions produced by long-held beliefs with a new story. At the time, and even on looking back at that sudden awareness, it seems a miracle. It also means I changed my frame of reference.

I have witnessed Rupa's transformation. She may not be as rich as her mother was, in actual cash flow, but she leads a rich and joyful life. And does the work and play she adores in several different areas, including leading groups and workshops internationally. She loves sacred and free form dance and whirls as a Sufi Dervish. Rupa also makes an impact helping people recognize how to learn to trust the wisdom that lies in their body, by compassionately connecting to the emotional stories deep within.

www.RupaCousins.com

In my seminars, I often talk about the sad truth that many well-todo parents control their children with money, getting them to choose the life they want for them, and promising they'll be rewarded when the parents are dead.

Moneylove Action Exercise

Rupa's story suggests some questions to ask yourself.

1. What was the message sent to you by your parents about work?

Did this make you look forward to growing up and "going to work." Did their message let you think that getting a college education and then getting a good, steady job, was the way to go?

2. What was the message you got about their generosity?

Did you feel you were free to ask for money when you needed or wanted some? Or did you feel you always had to come up with a good story to convince them to give you money? Did you feel taken care of by them, or encouraged to take care of yourself?

A Million Lost, a Life Found

Because it fits in so well in this section, I want to tell another story also never told before, of a couple who came to me for coaching because they wereseriously stuck in poverty consciousness, even though they were living well in a beautiful home. I'll call them Peter and Dana. For some years, they withheldgoing after their true passion, which was to make a difference in the world through their cooking and hospitality skills. They wanted to produce their own TV cooking show. The reason they delayed so long in going for their dream was thatDana's father was a rich man who controlled his family by giving and withholdingmoney, sort of a dance of temptation and fear. He had repeated a promise toDana on many occasions that when he died she would get control of a million dollars being held in trust for her. She and Peter put much of their lives on hold, thinking that million dollars would make everything so much easier. But her father's business manager had another plan in mind and stole all the money, including Dana's mother's inheritance. Dana and Peter were immobilized and devastated when this was revealed. They couldn't even imagine a solution.

I gave them some assignments. First to forgive Dana's father, for simply repeating a pattern he probably got from his father. And then, much harder, to forgive the business manager, who disappeared after absconding with the money.This was the most difficult part of their recovery. Whenever they thoughtabout the situation and what had happened, they indeed would experience a physical sensation of tightness, and shaking with anger and frustration and helplessness. It wasn't easy, but I gave them some tools and ideas to work with to confront the fact that they were still two very talented and good people whohad what it takes to be very successful. They got their cooking show shortly after that, which led to books, and then the founding of a nonprofit foundation to make a difference in the world through citizen diplomacy.

Moneylove Action Exercise What's Your Money Message?

If you're a parent, what messages are you sending about money and how easy or hard it is to produce? If you're a grandparent, how are your kids teaching your grandchildren that they should have a prosperity conscious attitude in life? Exactly what kind of thoughts are you projecting out into the world. Make a list of ten things you can remember recently saying or thinking about money.

Are the money messages you are delivering in congruence with the person you want to be in terms of a prosperous attitude?

More About Stanley, Monkey Mind, and Your Inner Pauper

What can I say about Dr. Maria Nemeth, clinical psychologist and coach's coach (many of the best of them train at her Academy of Coaching Excellence in

Sacramento, California) She is one of my favorite prosperity teachers, and her book, **The Energy of Money**, is a classic. She also wrote, **Mastering Life's Energies**. I've interviewed Maria at length because she is one of those people who always has some new ideas about old issues. Her in-depth look at the psychological issues around money, and both metaphysical and physical reality make many other prosperity books and programs look rather dull and shallow.

I was pleased to find out that what is exciting Maria right now is working with people to get rid of money worries. In the following monologue she gave to me (because I wouldn't dare interrupt her juicy flow to ask a question or make a comment), Maria Nemeth talks about money worries and fears in a way that exemplifies her bywords, Clarity, Focus, Ease, and Grace:

People are so worried about money nowadays, and I read an article recently saying that many people lie awake at night doing math tables in their heads. You know, "How much do I make an hour?" "How much of a raise do I need?" Most people didn't like to do math in school, and they certainly don't like to do math in their heads right now.

But that's one of the things that happens with money worries. I found in my own work with people, that worries about money sap so much creative energy. It's worrying about not having enough, "Am I going to make ends meet?", "Am I ever going to really be able to retire?" And this is what keeps people up at night.

My vision that I'm dedicated to is that people live worry-free when it comes to money. That they learn how to take worries, doubts, fears, off the table. Absolutely and completely off the table. All the worries that we have energize the amygdala. It's this little almond-shaped part of our brain and it's the seat of fight, flight, or freeze. Our brain has not significantly changed in 100,000 years, and it's designed to look for stress. To look for danger because that's how we survived. We didn't have fangs or fur, we couldn't run very far, but we had a brain, and we still have it, not appreciably changed since prehistoric times 100,000 years ago.

That brain looks for what could go wrong. Looks for all the stuff in life that could be a danger to us or a threat. So if you learn how to shift the focus of your attention from that aspect of your brain to something that is of interest, something that has true meaning for you, something that has true heart for you, something that you are grateful for--if you learn to focus your attention on those things, you can clear away all the worries, doubts, and fears--and 99.99 percent of them are imaginary. Mark Twain said, "I've had a lot of worries in my life most of which never happened." And that's true about us, we went through many, many difficulties, most of which never really happened.

When we look back on our lives, yes, we've had ups and we've had downs, but it's the anticipation of pain, it's the anticipation of having to live without, that's what saps our energy. I'm dedicating myself to giving people tools to shift their relationship with money and therefore move their life from scarcity to abundance.

www.acecoachtraining.com

We'll hear a lot more from Dr. Maria Nemeth and the energy of money, and the way to deal with difficulty when trying to move desires and dreams from the metaphysical reality to the physical reality in the upcoming Book Seven, **Building a Prosperous Spirit.**

Feeling Those Old Amygdala Blues

I think Maria did an amazing job of putting it all together, where the worries and fears come from, and how to start dealing with them. Yes, she agrees with me that drowning Stanley with lots of positive messages, is a way of diminishing his power over you, or the Monkey Mind, or the amygdala. Research has shown that the amygdala, which is part of the limbic system, has a large role in triggering fear. It is a major factor in what is called your lizard brain, and goes back to prehistoric times. It creates a lot of obstacles, especially when you are taking a risk or moving toward a major change. Noted writer and blogger, Seth Godin, says, *"Why did the chicken cross the road? Because her lizard brain told her to."* This is very much in line with what Maria Nemeth says, "Your lizard brain is here to stay and your job is to figure out how to quiet it and ignore it."

While I see my inner pauper, or Stanley, drowned in a sea of positive messages, activities, and people, Maria says:

"Focus on something that is of interest, something that has true meaning for you, something that has true heart for you, something that you are grateful for."

This is one big reason so many coaches and personal development teachers stress the importance of gratitude in our lives.

Moneylove Action Exercise The Three Gratitudes

Several spiritual teachers have recommended and taught me this.

It couldn't be more simple, but oh so powerful. Just make a list, either on paper or in your head every night before going to bed, of three things you are grateful for having, accomplishing, learning or enjoying that day.

Researchers have also found that the amygdala will calm down when you are experiencing great pleasure, or involved in something you are passionate about, be it a person or a creative project. You may not be able to see this little almond-shaped part of your brain, but you know when it is kicking and screaming and trying to block your forward momentum.

Moneylove Action Exercise

This one is pretty obvious. Think of a time when you were getting close to taking a risk that could bring you major positive results, but fear and worry shut you down. Answer the question:

What was my Monkey Mind or Amygdala or Inner Pauper or Stanley saying or doing to try to stop me in my tracks?

And if you can remember what was going on in your body, what your physical sensation was at that moment, so much the better.

Now think of a time when you took that risk, made that change, did the thing that got you closer to your dream and the results you wanted. Ask:

What was happening in my life? What was I doing with passion, with focused attention, that distracted my negative little voice and let me move past it?

Remember, most of our fears and worries about money are never realized, never happen. So ask yourself:

What was some serious worry or fear or anxiety I had about money that never came to pass, that I realize in retrospect was really not a likely possibility?

Realize that you own that little lizard brain part of you inside your head. It is real, but almost all of the things it feels threatened and endangered about are not. It's rather a simpleton, like a child really, and will respond easily to distractions, especially if they feel good, or put you on fire with passion

Rickie Moore, PhD

This chapter provided me with a lot of surprises, not the least of which was the serendipitous arrival of clinical psychologist and author, Rickie Moore, PhD, back into my life after 25 years. Thanks to Facebook, which she rarely visits or uses, she checked me out because a Dutch woman house-sitting in her Amsterdam home found a copy of Moneylove on a shelf and told Rickie she really liked it, which made Rickie wonder what had happened to me. When she saw a post about this new book, she got in touch to say she would love to be a part of it. She has created a formula for life and all its aspects that she hasn't yet gotten to write her own book about, and generously offered to let me share it here. How could I resist an offer like that? But I also got the bonus of a great story she has to tell and now you get it, too:

Rickie's Tale

I was teaching how to age gracefully, looking at what it is we're all searching for, and what does wealth mean.

And then I fell. I broke my back, and I broke my hip, and I got a hole in my eye and lost the sight in my left eye, so I lost my balance. So now I can only walk with my arm in somebody's arm, like my husband or a friend. I can walk a lot but I need to have help. And I'm still teaching aging gracefully. I have a better concept of how to live gracefully since this happened to me and everything in my life changed completely. And still, I'm the happiest person I know.

When I fell and thought I was going to be in a wheelchair and couldn't see, and they couldn't regulate the pain, I decided I wanted out of here. So I decided to check out. Happily, I live in a country where you can have help to leave.

I got really really clear. I said to myself, "You know, I have been teaching how to live, and now my next big teaching is how to leave." So I made all these arrangements to go. The will to live is a fabulous thing to lose. Because once you lose it, once you lose it and it comes back, life becomes clearer. You know, we hear all the rhetoric about, "Live every moment," and "Life is so precious." Maybe that's true, but you don't really get it until you lose the will to go on, and then, because I was blessed that it came back, it came back like lightning.

I got the message in the hospital one night. It said, "Rickie, you have lived, you've served your purpose, and now it's time to go home." My husband, Henry, came into the room and his response was, "Honey, I think what the message meant was come home to our home and to me."

So I realized that my challenge now was to help people understand how important it is to plan how to leave. That leaving is just as important as living. We have to learn how to leave this life with grace, and beauty, and even joy. To plan an exit where it's really special, and you're assisted, and you have it the way you want--it's very tempting and something to, in a sense, look forward to. And most of us are so frightened of death. This is what my accident did for me. I have no fear of dying.

On the other hand, I've never lived as fully. I mean I've always lived fully, completely, absolutely. I want to write a book about this formula I was given, that thousands of people are using, and I don't even have a book out on it. It's finding the time to do it, and also the time for joyful playtime.

Rickie Moore's Formula

It's called The Tri-Energetics Formula. Rickie calls it a holistic system involving the body, mind, and spirit. She says, "The fundamental of it is,"

First of all, ***Know What You Need. Say What You Want. Have Clear Intentions And Be:***

Flexible. Compassionate, and Curious.

Rickie says,

"It wasn't until recently that I realized how amazing this simple formula is. For example, people can look at their relationship. Say there's a quarrel or whatever. You can check on any one of these parts of the formula and say, "Oh, wait a second, it's the flexibility. That's what's missing. You're not being flexible." Or look at curiosity, and maybe you'll say, "No, you're being defensive, not curious." Or you can look at your health. The body needs flexibility. The spirit needs curiosity, otherwise everything is dogma. So every single aspect of it is a formula that allows you to look at, decipher, say "That's what's going on here." It may be your lack of curiosity, my lack of compassion. You follow the formula through whatever.

Until I lost the will to live and then got it back, I didn't get that this formula--this specific formula, is the most succinct guide to waking up there is. Just look at it. Because no one who doesn't know what they need. cannot say what they want, doesn't have clear intentions, is not

flexible, is not compassionate and/or curious--has ever woken up, ever. The formula is a guide to waking up. To awakening--being all you can be, it's being happy! It's living!

Rickie then surprised me (she has always been one of the most spontaneous people I've known) by starting to sing, in a deep lovely voice, the most recent of 250 songs she has written. She said, *"I wrote this when I was doing a very large master class in Germany."*

Wake up, wake up, know what you need, Wake up, wake up, say what you want, Wake up, wake up, with a clear intention to Live, Love, Laugh and Be Happy. Live, Love, Laugh and be happy. I'm up, awake, I'm flexible, I'm up, awake, compassionate I'm up, awake, and curious To Live, Love, Laugh, and Be Happy!

www.inpeacenet.com

Moneylove Action Exercise

Well, I already tried it out on an issue challenging me, and as I suspected, Rickie Moore is right. It is amazing. But it doesn't work if you just nod your head and say, *"That looks pretty interesting. Maybe I'll try it someday."* To again quote a friend of mine who has taught thousands of people to change their lives, *"Do the damn exercises!"*

Just take something that isn't going the way you would like right now, and apply the six criteria to see what's missing.

1. **Do you know what you need?**
2. **Have you said what you want?**
3. **Are your intentions as clear as they can be?**
4. **Are you being flexible enough?**
5. **Are you being compassionate?**
6. **Are you curious?**

I'll add one further question to the process.
7. **Are you ready for a breakthrough?**

It's true that I and some of my contributors have talked about several of these points, but I like the way Rickie has put these particular things together and I think you will like the results.

Barbara Winter

Barbara Winter, author of, **Making a Living Without a Job**, who you'll hear a lot more from in upcoming sections, brought up a good point for us to be aware of when looking at our poverty messages:

Sometimes we don't know what our negative beliefs may be. I had a big realization about my money beliefs one year when I went Christmas shopping in Santa Barbara, and everyone I saw looked like a mugger, so I had to go home. And I had a realization that I had a belief that I didn't know I had, which was, "If I have money, people will hurt me." And that was so huge, and the recognition of it. Sometimes those poverty conscious beliefs just sit there quietly and keep steering the ship.

Moneylove Action Exercise

Your homework assignment for this book is to write a sentence about prosperity and success. But write it as the person you would like to become. Write it as if it's something you would be happy to share with your family and friends, to encourage them and demonstrate that you really have upped your game and increased your prosperity consciousness, and are steering your own ship.

Book Five TimeLove

"All my possessions for a moment of time." Queen Elizabeth I, said with her dying breath in 1603.

Take your time reading this, because I really want you to understand I am not talking about managing your time, or being more efficient in its use, or even making it your friend instead of your enemy. These may all be part of the process, but I am declaring first and foremost that you have the power to change the way this manmade construct called time operates in your life, the power to bend it into submission to your desires and wishes, and be more flexible and playful and creative in your use of it.

TimeLove is intentionally written at a very contemplative, meditative pace--to give you more time to absorb it all.

Another unique aspect is that TimeLove has its own Appendix. An appendix is usually a section at the end of a book that has supplementary material that is related to the book's topic, but didn't necessarily fit in the regular format.

In this case, the TimeLove Appendix contains a lot of ideas and thoughts I've had about time in the past thirty-some years, but that I felt would have interrupted the particular tone and flow I wanted for this part. It contains some of my favorite concepts of time, but definitely is separate from the main book. You can decide for yourself whether this separation makes sense or not.

Understand one thing: this is not about time management, it is about time ownership. Would you rather be the manager of a business, reporting to a boss, or the owner of that business?

Most of the time management programs and teachers are operating on a very archaic and linear view of time, or as Martin Boroson puts it, a Newtonian view of time.

Sir Isaac Newton, who said the plague years of 1665-1667 were the most creative of his life, said about time: *Absolute, true, and mathematical time, in and of itself and of its own nature, without reference to anything external, flows uniformly and by another name is called duration. Relative, apparent, and common time is any sensible and external measure (precise or imprecise) of duration by means of motion; such as a measure—for example, an hour, a day, a month, a year—is commonly used instead of true time.*

If you choose to examine Sir Isaac's statement carefully, and realize that billions of people have been living by his definition made in the 17th Century, it will become apparent that, in this instance, he was a man of his time rather than one who was ahead of it. While he is acknowledged as the greatest scientist of that era, he was floundering about trying to describe something we have a much better understanding of after the 350 years of time which have passed since then.

I think a debate between Newton and Albert Einstein would have been exciting to see, as Einstein famously said, **"Time and space are modes by which we think, not conditions in which we live."** Can you imagine how much that profound truth about the relationship between human beings and time would have boggled Isaac Newton's mind? I find it interesting that Einstein kept a picture of Newton on his study wall.

But even though I quote two of the greatest scientists in human history, this is not about science, but rather a book that uses the history, philosophy, and psychology of time to come up with a new paradigm, a new perspective, a new way of achieving time-mastery.

As I said almost thirty years ago:

Time is something we have empowered with properties that have hampered our own creativity, success, prosperity, and freedom. Each of us has to make a choice as to whether to submit to enslavement by time or become its master.

We are locked into a certain pace in life based on perceptions of time handed down by significant others in our life, as well as generations of others since the Dawn of Time.

(No doubt, in saying this, I was ahead of my time.)

I'm not sure who said it, but a definition of the difference between rich and wealthy says: Rich is how much money you have, wealthy is about how well you live. My definition of prosperity is in alignment with the wealthy part of that equation, and how well you live has a lot to do with how you view and approach and use time.

Owning your time is about giving yourself permission to have a life that is filled with alternatives and joyful experiences, and loving relationships, and real freedom of choice. To further illustrate this difference between wealthy and rich, you might look at some rich people who spend sixty or eighty hours per week in the pursuit of making more money. Or you might look at one of the richest men in the world, Warren Buffet, who has said he only works three hours a day. Rich people often have the feeling that the accumulation of money is the be-all and end-all of life. Those who are wealthy and prosperity conscious, have instead understood all along that it's the quality of life which matters most.

Our Most Precious Natural Resource

It all boils down to this: The most important thing in all the world, and in your life is time. It is a natural resource far more valuable than diamonds, gold, or oil. Many people avoid this truth by thinking money is the most important thing. But money isn't important unless it buys you time, unless it gives you the freedom to take charge of your time, unless it gives you lots of pleasant things to do with your time.

The late comedian, George Carlin, would do a bit where he said, "There's a moment coming. Here it comes. Its getting closer. Its almost here. There it goes!"

Carlin went on to say, "There's no present. There's only the recent past and the near future."

And as with many of his humorous statements, this is the truth. If you are spending this moment remembering the last moment or anticipating the next moment, then this moment isn't a reality for you.

How Long Does It Take?

How long does it take you to do things? Does it really take you exactly forty hours to produce a weekly income? Fortunately, many people have let go of that myth. But a lot of people still believe that this is the ideal work week for them. It's an arbitrary figure set by accident because workers rebelled against sixty and eighty hour workweeks. In the 1920s, Henry Ford established the 5 day, forty-hour work week. It wasn't because there were so many industrial accidents because workers were exhausted, and it wasn't for the benefit of the workers, or for scientific reasons. It was because Henry Ford wanted his workers to have the leisure time to buy stuff, especially his cars.

Here's an important point to consider: If you don't enjoy your leisure time right now, if you don't have something that gives you pleasure or robust expectations during your time away from work, then you'll have little or no incentive to increase your free time.

"Free time," there's an interesting phrase. What does it mean? Time you don't pay for? Or time in which you have the freedom to do whatever you want? And is it really free time for you? Think about the next "free time" you have coming. It might be right now. Time when you don't have to be working. Are you really free to do anything you want with this time? You actually are, even if you don't accept it , even if you don't use it. You can do anything you want with this time, and, in fact, with any time you have. No one owns your time but you. Unless you give it away, unless you give other people the power to take your time away from you.

A Time Awareness Exercise

There will be many of these scattered throughout TimeLove and its Appendix, and your exploring your relationship to time by taking part in them will add to the value of your reading experience. This first one is an "Oldie but Goodie."

Through the years, one of the most popular Moneylove strategies was called simply, "The Thousand-Dollar-An-Hour Strategy". You start imagining that your time is worth a thousand dollars an hour--and no one else has to think this, only you. But when you start to conjure up the possibilities you'll realize that if your time was really this valuable, you would pay a lot more attention to how you use it. Think about this, if you were paying one thousand dollars just to read this one segment in this one book, wouldn't you be paying more attention, wouldn't you be more likely to use the information, to do the awareness and action exercises, to make the most of the time you are using to read it?

With a thousand-dollar-an-hour mentality, you won't waste as much time with people who are boring, negative, energy draining--not if your time is worth a thousand dollars an hour! And you'll start thinking more clearly about the work you do. If you are not now being paid a thousand dollars an hour, you'd better at least be enjoying it. So, right now, take a moment to think about your time being worth a thousand dollars an hour, and how it might affect the way you see and use time.

Time Awareness Exercise

Five Things Time Means to You

Can you come up with five personal statements as to what time means in your life? Take a few moments now to make a list of:

What Time Means to Me

Very rigid concepts of time permeate our lives. We're taught that it takes forty hours a week to produce a week's earnings, no matter how brilliant, talented, or creative we are.We're taught that it takes a certain amount of years to get an education, no matter how rapidly our brain can absorb new material. We're taught to equate experience with a long amount of time devoted to any single activity.

The reality is that some people can learn more in a week than others putting in thirty years. But the one putting in thirty years is considered "someone with experience." All of these beliefs are tied to the lowest common denominator of ability and intelligence. And they don't take into account the fact that the general population is now more sophisticated, more aware, and more intelligent than ever before in history. And we're still holding on to some of those ancient ideas about time.

A big difference between someone who earns $50,000 a year and someone who may earn $50,000 in a day, is that the person who earns $50,000 in a year doesn't believe it can be done any faster, in any less time.

Which Group Do You Belong In?

There are two basic attitudes about time that I want to mention. One is Newtonian, after Isaac Newton and it involves those people who work a rigid work week, 8 hours a day, 40 hours a week, These people keep their work and their leisure strictly separate. They are strongly time-oriented.

Even in their leisure, they need things to do and they often need help from leisure industries to fill up their leisure time.

On the other hand, Einsteinians, for Albert Einstein, are people who look for jobs with flexible work hours, or they create their own businesses. They believe that work and play are not essentially different. And they are oriented to their own rhythms in both work and play. They refuse to allow the clock to create leisure time for them. They create their own leisure time, which is not dependent on the clock.

My Personal Relationship with Time

One of the reasons I feel comfortable still teaching prosperity consciousness, while I am recovering from ending up broke and in prison, is that I am richer than almost anyone I know in what may be our most priceless asset, time. I have liberated, mastered, and owned time in my life to a great extent so that minutes and hours and days and weeks mean less to me than to most people. I moved to Panama and have declared it a Jerry Time-Free Zone.

I rarely make plans that force me to be somewhere at a certain time. A temporary aberration was the two months I have used to write this book, when I had to make appointments to do interviews around the world on Skype.

I get up when I want and go to sleep when I want, and almost always do what I want. If someone comes up with a wonderful offer to use time in a pleasant, interesting, or exciting way, I only need a moment's notice to join the party. I am a living testimonial to demonstrate that anyone can take charge and own the time in their life (and you certainly don't have to relocate to a new country), and it is very worthwhile to consider doing so, to be willing to do so, and to take action to make it happen. I was lucky in that I had many clues in my life that this was possible. That I could make up my own rules concerning time.

Punctual to a Fault

Ironically, despite my freewheeling approach to time, which extends to very flexible sleep cycles and mealtimes, I am punctual to a fault. I think this stems from my 12 years as a radio broadcaster. If I showed up late for that job, someone would be on the microphone instead of me, and there was always the danger that the boss would think they were doing a better job. But I like the fact that I always show up early or on time for every appointment or event or social engagement. Here in Panama, where tardiness is a national sport, it has sometimes been a challenge, but I always bring my Kindle stocked with a good mystery novel in case I am having to wait in an empty room for a few minutes.

Many writers, some of them very successful, told me it took at least a year to write a nonfiction book. I wrote **Moneylove** in a little over two weeks. I had a three month deadline, but as is often the case, I procrastinated until the last 18 days. Of course, I had by that time been talking about the Moneylove principles for about a year, as well as doing workshops on the subject, so I did know my material, but even my editor was surprised, as very few authors consistently meet their deadlines.

Boggling, Bending, and Action

TimeLove presents some mind-boggling, time-bending concepts, along with action steps if you would like more personal ownership of your time. For this, I have a partner in talking about and teaching prosperity time consciousness. You are very fortunate that I discovered him and got him to share so much of his insights about time and how we use it. You'll meet him in a moment (no pun intended, though you'll soon discover there could have been.)

My mission statement for TimeLove, is to get you to think about time and how you use it and possibly abuse it in your life. We are operating on a system of time that originated with some mythological period we often call The Dawn of Time. But times and time itself have changed. Throughout the world, more and more people of imagination are molding time to suit their own desires and needs.

I really believe every single prosperity teacher, motivational speaker, life coach and therapist has gotten it wrong up to now. Including me. Our focus has been on the wrong thing when we have talked about making more money, having better relationships, even living a healthier life. At the essential core, the bottom line, the true secret of life, the meaning of all things, lies TIME, that component we have built a whole set of facades and functions around, in effect, constructing a manmade prison that restricts, limits, and confines us.

One of my favorite quotes has always been Christopher Morley's:

"There is only one success, to be able to spend your life in your own way.

And think about what this is saying, for it is all about time, spending your time the way you want to spend it as the ultimate human success story.

As to money, its only real value is in being able to exchange it for time you can use doing what you want to do. Relationships are about spending that time with the people you want to spend it with. Health is about having your time unencumbered by illness and unlimited by a shortened lifespan as well as having the energy to make full use of your time.

Most people are sure money is more important than time, and that all they have to do is create enough extra money and time will take care of itself. A less true assumption has rarely been perpetrated or adopted. And here's a shocking revelation:

Time is not about mathematical calculations and measurements as Newton declared. It is about emotional events and episodes. This may be the most important statement for those who want to escape the tyranny of time:

Time is ruled by emotions and beliefs rather than the clock.

Passion Rules Time

Passion trumps the clock in assessing the value of time. The most valuable and precious time we experience is contained in those moments when we are so passionately engaged in some aspect of our lives that we lose our very sense of time and its passing. We all have had those moments, and for me, the true secret of a happy, successful, and fulfilling life is to have as many of those timeless experiences as possible. For most of us, these moments happen by happy accident. But I am suggesting that we can control this and create a life containing a lot more of them, a lot more time in which we lose track of time.

There are people who never have enough time to do all they want, and there are those who have too much time on their hands and are bored because they can not think of anything to engage or excite them.

One perceptual approach to mastering time is to enjoy having more things to do and experience and absorb and learn and know than you have time for--to feel like the master of your universe because you have so many pleasing and productive choices and get to select from among them and put others on the back burner of your consciousness.

It all comes down to this: time itself has no significance. What truly matters is how you use it, what you do with it, and the role you let the mechanical or electronic ticking of the clock or watch dictate how you live your life.

An Aside

(Do I have time for an aside here? It doesn't matter because I'm going to take the time!)

One of the most powerful messages millions of people in the U.S. and around the world got about the nature of time came quite innocently, two generations ago, and is still affecting the ideas about time many people are carrying around inside their heads. Starting as a radio newscast, and much more significantly, becoming a movie newsreel called The March of Time.

From 1935 to 1951 could be called the golden era of movies, when they were the main entertainment and recreational experience in most people's lives.

And when people went to the movies, they would see the March of Time newsreel in addition to the main film attraction, with the deep throated announcer, Westbrook Van Voorhis, proclaiming at its conclusion in a somewhat ponderous way: "Time ....Marches On!" I imagine few people hearing that, and the many who tried to imitate Van Voorhis's voice saying this to entertain their friends, realized how powerful and insidious a message about the nature of time was being programmed into their subconscious minds. And if your parents or grandparents saw The March of Time on a regular basis, they may have very well passed on the message of time marching away from us, very regimented and intense.

Might I suggest that rather than seeing time marching on, you consider time as dancing on and you get to choose the dance it does, whether its a foxtrot, American swing, romantic tango, lively salsa. slow and lovely waltz. Whatever dance and pace you choose, rather than the boring, consistent image of marching feet. And whatever you do in life, do enjoy the dance.

Columnist, sociologist, and best-selling author, Martha Beck, obviously agrees and has written about what she calls The Tyranny of Time:

Our clocks, our calendars, our associations drive us like overburdened pack mules from one hurried task to another. One of the most essential tasks for living a life of purpose and joy is to command your time, rather than let it command you.

Martha Beck also has advice similar to mine for when time seems to overwhelm you and the people around you have a problem with your more flexible scheduling choices, she says you should put on some music and, *"Start dancing!"*

This also reminds me of something the late poet and spiritual teacher, Ric Masten, said, "If you could slow time down enough, you would see that the mountains are dancing."

Not only do most people not know how to begin mastering time, most haven't a clue that it is even possible to change our relationship to the powerful force in our lives, which can be insidious and destructive, or nurturing--depending on how we see it, what we believe about it, and how we have been programmed to use it in our lives.

Time Getting In the Way

Where time gets in the way and becomes more of an obstacle than the valuable tool it was invented to be is when we misperceive it, allow it to restrict us.

For example, for many people, the quantity of time they have is more important than the quality. Someone will die at fifty after a life filled with accomplishments, with every day and every hour an example of a purposeful, impactful, useful, and fulfilling life. And many people will talk about the pity of it all, that this person died so young. While someone who lives until 90 in a life that was not nearly so well-lived, enjoyable, or useful--we celebrate by saying, "What a wonderful, long life."

We miss the point completely about the gift of life. In the larger scheme of things, we are all here for an instant, a moment if you will, whether its twenty years or fifty or 110. How well we live our individual days and hours and even minutes dictates the success or failure of that life, not a final tally of how many minutes, hours,and days went by.

Most of the timesaving devices invented over the past hundred years haven't saved time for most people. We are locked in to old ideas that keep us imprisoned in a sort of time warp, a place where time goes by too fast or too slow depending on which can do us the most damage, while it is possible to have it go by fast or slow to meet our needs and desires.

We can choose to mold time to our own desires and purposes. In simple terms, to slow time down when we're experiencing good things, like creativity, joy, love, fulfillment, and speed time up when whatever is occurring is not so pleasant or productive.

The mastery of time can put your life into a more effective mode of manifestation.

I've always said a task will take as much time as you devote to it. But its original form was **Parkinson's Law**, the adage that "work expands so as to fill the time available for its completion."

This was created by Cyril Northcote Parkinson as part of the first sentence of a humorous essay published in *The Economist* in 1955. He was a former British civil servant (no surprise there).

I want to make note here that the slow unwrapping of this portion of **Moneylove 3.0** has been intentional, not to test your patience, but to give you a sense of the value of slowing time down and preparing your mind to take in new ideas. Some of the most essential and juiciest stuff about time is coming up. As well as action-specific exercises to explore your own perceptions and boundaries around time, and give you tools to change any of those that aren't serving you well.

A Semester With the Professor of Time

TimeLove is formatted a bit differently than most parts of most books. The reason was dictated by circumstances, and happily so. As is true for most writers of nonfiction books, I planned to pick and choose from comments recorded during interviews with the various experts I wanted to share with you. But most of these are much more than experts, they are people who have mentored me, or said things that changed my perspective on things. So these are very personal connections for me, and I wanted to give you a taste of that.

In the case of Martin Boroson, it would have been easy to just take some excerpts from his comments about time and include them with my own ideas. However, he said so many profound things during our series of one hour interviews, that I decided to share most of it as he said it, whole and intact. Though unusual, I think it adds tremendous value to TimeLove.

This is like an entire semester of a course on the philosophy, psychology and history of time, including specific action steps you can use to change your own perception and use of time. If you pay attention (and to borrow a phrase from prosperity master, Edwene Gaines, "If you are teachable.") your thoughts and beliefs about time are about to be challenged and changed forever. Is that something worth spending your valuable time on to achieve?

Author's Note:

To make it easier to differentiate during times Martin and I went rapidly back-and-forth, I have identified which of us is speaking and put Martin's quotes and comments in italics.

Martin Boroson is the author of One Moment Meditation, and he has been thinking about the concept of a moment for many years.

Jerry:

Why do you feel a moment is so significant in the realm of time?

Martin:

I think the whole secret to time ownership and the way we can expand time in a prosperous way, rather than in a punitive, negative or stressed-out way--I think the whole secret of that lies in the "moment."

When writing <u>One-Moment Meditation</u>, I looked up what the word moment actually meant, and discovered that it comes from a Latin word that means, "a particle sufficient to turn the scale." The moment was actually a very small weight, and when

131

you put the moment on a scale, it tipped the balance. I found this remarkable because it suggests that something very, very, very small can have an enormous consequence. In other words, the moment is an experience in which everything can turn around. The moment is like a tipping point, an experience in which anything can happen.

Jerry:

So a moment has impact and depth and meaning beyond and irregardless of the amount of actual physical time that goes by?

Martin:

Yes. A moment is actually not a unit of time. It is an experience beyond time. Consider life-changing moments. These are times when an unexpected reversal occurs. We were headed in one direction, in a linear way, and then something happened that suddenly changed things. But whether we judge these to have been positive or negative, what they have in common is that something unpredictable happened, something momentous happened, and it didn't take time. So in life-changing moments, we see the dramatic property of a moment.

Time Is Not a Physical Reality

If you look at the philosophy, the history, and the physics of time, there is no agreement about what time is. Physicists and philosophers don't know what time is. And some physicists actually say that time doesn't exist at all, that it's a construct that human culture, the human mind, has created. It's something we're carrying in our minds that doesn't actually relate, in any direct way, to something in the physical universe.

There's no property of "time" as we conceive it in the physical universe. That is shocking to most people because we take time so literally. We think that because our wristwatch says three o'clock, there's a three o'clock somewhere out there in the universe. But when you study the physics and philosophy of time, you realize that there is no three o'clock. Einstein said, "Time and space are modes in which we think, not conditions in which we live."

We carry around time as if it were real, and forget that it is a collective construct. For example of how differently it can be constructed: There was a period in France in which they always had twelve hours of daylight and twelve hours of darkness, no matter what the time of year. They achieved this by varying the length of an hour. So, in the summer, they had just twelve "hours" of daylight. In other words, they had a very eccentric way of constructing time; but this one didn't find favor and died out.

Nowadays, we have a construct of time that is generally accepted around the world, that most people abide by. This is really useful because if you want to make an appointment, or you want to get to work when other people get to work, you need a common agreement about what time is. But we've gone way overboard in our belief that it's a hard-wired part of reality.

Jerry:

There were just a few all-night places in the 1970s and 1980s. I remember suggesting in my Moneylove Seminars back in the 1980s that a smart idea for an entrepreneur would be to copy what a San Diego print shop near the University of San Diego did, stay open 24 hours. That was a wild and crazy idea then, but very common now, as it is for supermarkets, convenience stores, restaurants, etc.

Martin:

Well, in a way, we may be evolving to a world like that, in that we are now open for business 24/7. I have clients in England, India, California, New York, and Australia, so my workday on the computer has gotten very long, but I can't possibly be there all the time. So, does it matter anymore "when" we work? Does it really matter when we sleep? I'm not saying that these changes are necessarily good, just that we are going to have to adapt to a new experience of time.

For example, I know a lot of people who wake up in the middle of the night and get very distressed that they're awake, but it may be their natural rhythm. And that time around 3 am when you wake up can be a tremendously creative or contemplative time, which makes me wonder: What would happen if we trusted that?

Our current understanding of time, and our understanding of business, comes from a more mechanical era when business was about how many units you could produce in a certain amount of time, and you got paid based on the number of hours you put in. You punched a clock. Or you got paid based on the number of units you produced.

Time For Idea People

That still happens, of course, but more and more people are working in a field where what matters is not the amount of time they put in, but the quality of their ideas. An "idea person," a creative person, has a very different experience of time than does a factory worker.

An idea person knows that if you wake up at 3 o'clock in the morning with a great idea, you'd better start working on it right then when the energy's up. Because that's when you're on fire, that's when the inspiration is coming through. This may mean that you have to sleep late the next morning and don't get to work on time. But if your employer really wants to benefit from your middle-of-the-night creativity, they had better let you come in late.

"Crazy Busy"

Unfortunately, the biggest change happening now--it's really a crisis-is that most people feel so incredibly busy. The first word out of a person's mouth when you ask, "How are you?" is "Busy." They feel overwhelmed. They also use the term, "crazy busy."

We live in an era in which we have an incredible number of timesaving devices: dishwashers, power mowers, vacuum cleaners, microwave ovens, cars, and computers; and yet, nobody has any time. So, we really must pause to conclude that something's not working.

If you really wanted to have more time, you would have to go to a pre-industrial culture and throw away your cellphone and computer and all your time-saving devices. Yes, you would have to chop your wood by hand, and grow your own food and wash your clothes in the river. Your days would be full, but I don't think you'd feel "crazy busy."

Why is this? When you do manual labor, by which I mean all those mindless chores that timesaving devices save you from doing, you have a chance to release or process what's in your mind--the conversations you had, a project you were struggling with, a difficult exchange you had with somebody. Or, with other kinds of manual labor, you have to focus on what you're doing or you'll get hurt. But even that gives you some mental clearing, because you're not *thinking about all those other things; you're getting a break from mental activity.*

But nowadays, as soon as we save time because of these wonderful timesaving devices, we fill that time with more mental activity. We go on the Internet, we check our emails, we get some more work done. We're filling the time we save with more mental stimulation. So, it's not that we don't have time, it's that our minds don't get any space.

So, I'm starting to think we are not crazy because we're busy; we're busy because we're crazy. In other words, we're not giving our minds a chance to unwind. This is why I believe, and what I'm teaching with One-Moment Meditation®, that if you can learn to meditate quickly, to clear your mind in a moment, this may be one of the best things you can do for yourself. This is especially true on those days when you think you don't have time; if you take just one moment to meditate, your day will feel more spacious ... because your mind will be more spacious.

If you consider carefully those days when you feel crazy busy, I think you will realize that so many things you are doing in that day that are not really necessary to do, and they just get you mentally wound up.

So, if you just liberated some of that time for your own peace of mind, you wouldn't feel so crazy busy. And if meditation isn't for you, you could just play ping pong or run around the block, or whatever. Just use some of that time to clear your mind. Then you'll go back to what you really have to do with a fresh perspective, with greater ease, with more energy, with greater clarity, and you'll probably get it done more quickly.

Jerry:

It's sort of like when you're eating at a fine restaurant, with many courses, they'll bring some sherbet to cleanse your palate, and then you start fresh and you can appreciate the new flavors of the next course much more intensely and enjoyably.

Martin:

I'm convinced that people can reclaim time in this way. It used to be that the whistle would blow at the end of the workday and you'd go home, but now <u>we</u> have to blow the whistle. We're in charge of our own whistle and we have to learn to get a grip on time.

You know, back when companies first stopped people from smoking in the office, but there were still a lot of smokers, people would go out in front of the building to take a smoking break. Okay, it was still an unhealthy habit, but at least it gave people a real break—a moment in which to reflect. Nowadays, you don't get that at all. No breaks. And even if you do take a break, you probably use it to check your cellphone.

So one of the things I do now is help companies set up environmental

cues to remind people to take a break. And there's a difference between a high quality break and a low quality break. A high quality break is meditating or playing, or giving somebody a hug, or breathing in some fresh air, or laughing with someone. A low-quality break involves filling your mind with useless or scary information.

A Bounty of Time

You can have all the money in the world and it doesn't buy you time if you don't choose to give yourself time. You can buy yourself all kinds of stuff, you can even have staff, and still not have any time, if you don't make the psychological shift I'm talking about. But if you make the shift, then you can experience a bounty of time.

I created an exercise to help with this that I call The Bonus Minute. It's advanced training in One-Moment Meditation, but here's the basic idea: It's a minute of meditation that you do as soon as you realize that you have just saved a little time.

Say you arrive at work early because the traffic is a bit less congested than you expected. Take a minute of that time you've saved to clear your mind with meditation. Or, if you're sending an email to someone and you realize, "Gosh, it would have taken me so long to write that by hand, address an envelope, put a stamp on it, and then bring it to the post office," take just one minute of that time you saved to enjoy how much time you now have. With this exercise, you'll find that there's lots of time in your day to clear your mind. And if you use some of those moments to clear your mind, you'll experience your whole day as more spacious--and that's prosperity.

In other words, time becomes something that you can enjoy. It becomes something that you can give, something that you can play with--that you can indulge in.

Energy, time, and money are related. If you feel that you don't have enough time, if your perception of your life is that you are running short of time, sooner or later you will run out of energy, because it's an exhausting state of mind to maintain.

Time is something we have empowered with properties that can hamper our own creativity, success, prosperity, and freedom, if we're not careful. Give yourself permission to live your own life with your own time. Look at some of the *rigid perceptions about time, and whether you rule time or it rules you.*

In a work environment, people often feel embarrassed about taking personal time off, as if we're not entitled to personal time. We always have to be operating on company time, or government time, or time imposed by societies and cultures. While humans created time, we have largely given up control of it.

No matter how broke you are, you can change your experience of time. Personally, the times in my life when I've been the most broke, I've had the most time. And I really enjoyed that time. I didn't like being broke, of course, but I really enjoyed the time. And the things I did when I was broke, that didn't cost much, like write and read and play the guitar, gave me a lot of joy. That taught me something.

Jerry: I see that as a sign that someone really has prosperity consciousness, when they can still enjoy their time while they're broke, or between jobs, or deeply in debt.

Martin: *The people who lived in pre-industrial cultures had very little free time. They spent their days farming or cleaning or hunting. Their days were full, and their survival depended, in an immediate way, on most of the things they were doing. But I will bet you that they didn't feel <u>busy.</u> Ultimately, the responsibility to get a grip on time—to get a grip on the way we experience time—is ours. If we want to reap the benefits of living in the modern world, we have to reclaim time.*

Jerry:

So it's really not so much about time itself as it is about our individual perception of time. And it extends to our perceptions about life itself.

Martin:

To go back to where we started, Jerry: When you're truly present in that experience I call "the moment,"--when you're totally engaged in something you love doing--what happens is that you forget about time. You lose awareness of time. And you also lose awareness of yourself. You lose your self-consciousness. And the more you are "in the moment," the more you free yourself from the madness of time.

As part of the training I offer in One-Moment Meditation, I suggest that the best time to meditate is exactly at the moment you think, "I'm too busy to meditate." Meditate immediately when your whole psychological structure is saying, "Help--I'm too busy!" That's the moment of greatest opportunity. The training is to realize that even in that moment of extreme busyness, you can say, "I can stop."

You know, it's so easy to unwind when you're on vacation--nobody needs help with that. The challenge—and opportunity—is to do it when you're busy.

Jerry:

What about dreams? Sometimes if I wake up with a very clear memory of what my dream entailed, it's a whole adventure, a quest I went on that seemed like it lasted days, even weeks. And since I woke up earlier, then went back to sleep, had the dream, then woke up yet again, I can measure that only eight minutes went by during which I had that dream. And it seems impossible, but my mind has created this whole complex scenario in a very small amount of time, and I've often wondered:

"What if we could capture that sort of control over time in our waking states?"

Martin:

If you look at dreams, or other examples of what we call non-ordinary states of consciousness, whether they're accessed using meditation, yoga, psychedelics, drumming, or trance work—those states of consciousness that many people would call spiritual, healing, or creative or instructive—one of the common features of all of them is that our sense of time is very different than it is in ordinary consciousness. And almost always the experience is that so much more happens, or seems to happen, in those experiences than we imagine could happen in that amount of clock time.

So, there's no question, in my mind, that our higher functions can achieve a lot more in less time than we think. Or it might be more accurate to say that we can do these higher functions without time or beyond time. It's as if we've left someone behind on the ground measuring conventional time with a clock, while in those other states we are operating outside of time—maybe in another dimension. So, although we believe that the most important things take a lot of time, maybe they take no time at all.

In other words, what I realized, what led me to create One-Moment Meditation, is that we can jump to the essence of that. We can access these higher functions right now, because they don't take time. We can find them in just a moment.

This is so important for innovation. How much time does it take to have an idea? How much space does an idea require? An idea doesn't take up any time or space, but can have huge implications in the realm of time and space. So if you want to be innovative, you have to learn to be in the moment, to be outside time.

Jerry:

There's poverty time consciousness: a belief that there's never enough time to do what you want to do or what you have to do. Then there's prosperity time consciousness which is: "I decide how I want to use my time, and what needs to get done gets done when I say it gets done and I can pause and smell the roses whenever I choose to do so--I'm in charge." It's a really different attitude and it does dictate to some extent, how successful someone's life is and certainly how successful it feels while you're living that life.

We talk a lot about the quality of time without really doing much about it. There's so much talk about quality time and so little action aimed at making time have high quality.

Martin:

We must realize that our experience of time is what we make of it, and the next step is to realize that we actually create time. Then we realize that that we have the power to enjoy the illusion of time, that time isn't the enemy, and that we have the power to give time creatively.

When you have "prosperity time consciousness," you feel free to give and bestow time. You don't have a sense that there's a shortage of time, you don't have that sense of feeling crowded. You have a sense that you are living your time as you want to live it, sometimes maybe bending time, and at other times, accepting time as it is.

Jerry:

So we could say that prosperity is experiencing your whole day as spacious.

Playing With Time

Martin:

Well, certainly that's a good definition of prosperity time consciousness. Again, we live with a very Newtonian conception of time. We believe that time is measured, that time exists in the universe in a very mechanistic way, as if there were a clock in the universe, ticking. And because we have this view of time as objective and mechanical, which comes from Newton and clock technology, we forget that time actually is experienced much more subjectively. But when we're aware that time is experienced subjectively, and that it is a construct, we have a few more options within time—to expand it, to contract it, to find more of it.

As a friend once told me, "if you don't play with time, it plays with you." I think the ability to play with time is an ability we are certainly developing, culturally. I think you can see this in the more advanced companies where they understand the value of play and flexibility.

The old Newtonian companies are very much based on "Time is money." The number of pieces you produce in a given amount of time is your "value," so you punch in at the start of your day and you punch out at the end of your day and your employer wants to know how many units you assembled in that period of time. That's the old Newtonian understanding of time and business.

The new understanding of time in business is that it's flexible, and creative. So companies like Google will give their employees a certain percentage of their work day that is considered theirs to play with. Because Google knows that value will come out of that.

Some companies reward people based on their output not on their input, so however you manage to get the job done is up to you. You don't have to be sitting at your desk from 9 to 5. This is an attitude that says, here's what we need to achieve in this year, or this month. Whether you want to do that at midnight or eight in the morning, or at your desk or on the couch, or in the gym or wherever doesn't matter, just get it done--your way. This method acknowledges that people have different ways of getting the job done and in this way, time becomes more subjective and individual.

Remember, a single idea can have enormous value. And how long does an idea take? It doesn't take time. So when companies measure employees based on how much time they put in, that is antithetical to the idea of creativity and innovation. But if you want to liberate innovation and new thinking, you have to develop a more playful understanding, or a more flexible understanding of time.

People who are more creative do have a more flexible, playful understanding of time. When I was writing plays, there were some people who would imagine me sitting at a desk with a pen all day long. But, actually, I'd be cooking, singing, cleaning, doing all kinds of other things that don't look like writing, and of course, in this time, I was reflecting and creating. The actual writing down was only a very small amount of time.

Nowadays, when I really want to unblock my creativity, I create mini-retreats for myself. I tell everybody I'm not home. The phone's off the hook, I get in all my food so I don't have to go out of the house. I lay out a big roll of lining paper on the table, and I put out lots of crayons and things I want to play with. I then ask myself a question, the core question of the retreat. And then I let go of time.

I also let go of any requirements about what to do with my day. And by letting go of those requirements, I can follow the creative energy as it manifests in me. So this means that if it's three in the morning and I wake up on fire with an idea, I don't have to think, "Better get back to sleep because I have to get up and go to work in the morning."

You know, when people have an idea but say, "I'd better put it away because the time isn't right," that is murder to their creative impulse.

For the creative spark, the time is always right; the issue is whether you let yourself respond to it.

Jerry:
What would be a good starting point for someone who wants to change their relationship with time, become more flexible, more playful?

Martin:

The first thing is to try not to fill all your gap moments with the Internet or mobile devices. That's the biggest negative thing that's happening in our modern relationship to time. Whenever we have a minute free, we're filling it with more mental activity.

And then try to do something healthy that doesn't take long, that you can do in those gap minutes, whether it's ten jumping jacks, a minute of meditation, or sticking your head out the window to get some deep breaths of fresh air. If you've got a minute between things, do something healthy, rather than something numbing and distracting. And, rather than seeing these exercises as wasting time, see them as giving you a profound refreshment of your point of view.

As you have seen in Martin's comments, his ideas about time are ideas whose time has come.

You can find out more about Martin Boroson's keynotes and reflections at:

http://MartinBoroson.com

For specific training in One Moment Meditation® and a free video on how to do it:
http://OneMomentMeditation.com

As I listened to, and later read Martin's great stuff, several exercises popped into my head, as well as some further thoughts. I didn't want to interrupt his flow, so saved them for here and now.

Time Awareness Exercise

Reflect On a Life-Changing Moment

To assist yourself in understanding what Martin Boroson calls "the remarkably dramatic quality of a moment," actually do what he suggests and reflect on a life-changing moment right now. A moment in your life in which things seemed to completely turn around for you. This can be something that is good or bad. Or it can even be something that changed over time.

For instance, being fired from a job might seem bad in the immediate timeframe, but could easily turn into something good as you explore other talents and opportunities available to you. And if anything like this is true for you, can you also tune into the moment when it changed again?

Life's one certainty is change, and how you react and respond to it determines, to a great extent, how it goes. And many, perhaps most of those changes, do happen in a moment.

We have this limiting belief that it takes a certain specific amount of time to do certain things, and if we free up that construct when we're in that zone, it will probably amaze us at how much we can accomplish in very little time.

Things are moving much faster now, especially in the age of the computer and the almost universal acceptance of the Internet as the main form of exchange of information, with its nanosecond capacity to deliver that information. To take a wild speculative leap: what if we had an International Commission on Time and came up with a new construct to fit 21st century needs?

Maybe putting two days into each 24-hour period. Sure, this would be a shock after accepting the same parameters of time and agreeing to it for so many years, but can anyone doubt that we could come up with a better, newer model today?

Are You Willing to Experiment?

Here might be a good place and time for you to think about whether you would be willing to experiment with a total new construct of time in your life.

Time Awareness Exercise.

Pick a 24 hour period and play with imagining that it contains two full days. I have done this, by going to sleep at midnight, getting up at 4 in the morning and working at my computer, then going back to sleep at 10am until 2 or 3 in the afternoon. Then I wake up and perhaps have a second breakfast, then do some kind of creative work until 7pm, when I might relax and watch one of my favorite movie genres, British mysteries, on YouTube, or get together with friends, attending a concert or go dancing or out for a meal, then get back to bed at midnight.

Of course, you can structure your double-your-days experience any way you choose. If you are willing to try this on for size, you might want to take a period at the end of it to think about your feelings of having this kind of major change in your life. What about it do you like and what doesn't work for you at all?

It seems to me that this archaic common agreement about time is very similar to the common agreement we have about what money is and how much buys what. Money only works if everyone agrees that a hundred dollars is worth just so much, and can be exchanged for a certain amount of goods or services.

We're told that we use just a small portion of our brain's capacity, and if we put attention on developing some more of that brain power into focusing on how we can perceive time differently and have time function differently in our lives, we might be able to do some amazing things we've never before thought possible, or we've never even thought of thinking about.

Time Awareness Exercise

Take a period of time when it is possible and appropriate for you to put away all devices that measure time. As Martin suggests, see how it feels not to be aware of the minutes ticking away. You might have a whole different view of the nature of time, or you might find out how dependent you are on watching the watch or clock or time on your smartphone.

Time Awareness Exercise

Meditating On an Object

I think Martin is spot on about the merits of meditating. Personally, I like meditating on an object. Focusing on my senses.

Many years ago, I had a beautiful jade rubbing stone in a silk pouch and before I would do anything eventful or creative or in a situation where I was looking for a successful outcome or was nervous, I would take out that jade stone and just hold it and rub it. I rubbed it maybe for just thirty seconds. And it had a calming effect. It allowed me to empty my mind for that moment. And even if I just touched it for a moment, it was a sensual experience that replaced a bunch of thoughts going in and out.

Meditating on an object--it doesn't really matter what you use, but I think it helps if you have your senses involved, whether you're listening to something, tasting something, touching something or looking at something.

But the ritual part of it I think is important so that you repeat it and it becomes comfortable and familiar and a way of taking your mind off everything else going on for just that moment. A perfect ritual and meditating object, I strongly suggest, is a hundred dollar bill.

My Favorite Object to Meditate On

Take a hundred dollar bill and just carry it around, and whenever you have one of those gap moments, take it out and study it. You might even look up some of the significance of various parts of the design. See if you can notice how it feels different in different places on the bill. If you want to involve your thoughts and imagination, think about how long it takes to earn $100 in your life right now, and by how much you would like to shrink that amount of time.

If you can use a hundred dollar bill as a calming, meditation object, it will impact not only your ability to take charge of those extra moments that show up every day of our lives, but it will start to reduce any residual anxiety or negative feelings you might have about money.

Time Awareness Exercise

I think now would be a good time for you, the reader, to consider whether you actually know when in your normal 24-hour day you get the most useful and creative and profitable ideas. It might be useful for you to keep a Creative Time Journal for a month, keeping track of when those ideas are most likely to occur. This will allow you to know when to give yourself the time and space to just relax and think, reflect and contemplate. There's an excellent chance that, like most of us, you've missed out on some wonderful ideas by not having room in your busy life or your cluttered mind to allow them to blossom.

150

The good news is we are living in a more enlightened time in that more and more people are working from home where they can choose their hours.

You've probably realized by now that I'm pretty impressed with Martin Boroson, and one of the big reasons why is that he walks his talk. He doesn't only talk about changing our perceptions of time, but invented a whole new way of looking at meditation and how long it takes to do.

Just changing your frame of reference, your old beliefs and habits around time, can dramatically and very quickly change your life, your prosperity, and your energy and feeling of self empowerment.The more ways you discover to look at time, the more flexible your thoughts will be on the subject. TimeLove could be called a total immersion in some very new concepts around time, and therefore you probably have some new perceptions about time just from having read it. But if you now read it out loud, and follow other suggested instructions from the Instruction Manual, you can create a new way time operates in your life, and a way that you have much more control over. Since time was made by humans, you can remake it in your own image.

Each minute or hour that you take charge of becomes a stimulant for momentum in your life.

TimeLove Appendix

I'm going to open this Appendix (sounds a bit surgical, doesn't it?) with a proven powerful and effective strategy I copied exactly from *The Moneylove Manifesto*, the 38 page ebook thousands of people have downloaded free from http://MoneyLoveBlog.com/. It's not precisely about time awareness, which is why it's here, and I will add my current thoughts on the strategy following the original piece.

The Ninety Day Trial Period

*"This is perhaps the simplest strategy I've ever created, and one of the most powerful, as is often the case with simple solutions. It is one I recommended and talked about in many seminars over the years since **Moneylove** was first published. It helps with the main task of choosing which selections you make from the huge supply of information now thrown at us on an unending basis morning, noon, and night. But it also helps to build a muscle you absolutely need if you are going to be successful in any aspect of life: your decision-making muscle.*

*I first suggested in **Moneylove** that being able to make a decision quickly and firmly was a major key to success. And that pondering a long time over most decisions meant that even someone else making a bad or wrong decision could do so, deal with the results, and make a new decision based on more accurate information--all while you still might be considering that original decision.*

Becoming "The Decider" In Your Life

George W. Bush liked to call himself "The Decider". History will probably have some strong opinions on that, but it is a good term for you to be able to apply to yourself. Are you "The Decider" in your life?

Most indecision is due to one's uncertainty about one's judgment. And here is a way to easily deal with all that, and train yourself to increasingly be able to become "The Decider."

The strategy is to make every important decision in your life a probationary one, lasting just 90 days. If you can't decide whether a job offer is the right one for you, take the job, but plan on quitting after 90 days if it isn't feeling right. One friend of mine decided on a whole new career after she gave it a 90 day trial period.

Of course, some decisions will reveal themselves to you as bad ones in a lot less time, and you can reverse course when that happens. But 90 days seems to be a good amount of time to be able to assess any path you choose. I usually do the 90 day trial period with any new project I take on. And I don't have to feel guilty or like a quitter if I give up on that particular effort. After all, I was only giving it a 90 day trial.

And when it comes to acquiring information, getting some entrepreneurial or Internet training for instance, you definitely should know whether the material is valuable in 90 days or less.

I subscribed to one newsletter that I thought would prove helpful. But after 90 days, I found I was only reading small portions of it, so I cancelled. It hadn't passed the 90 day trial.

And another one of those provocative, some would say downright incendiary, Jerry Gillies philosophical principles: give anyone new in your life the same 90 day trial. If being with that person hasn't resulted in feeling good about yourself, sharing some happy experiences, or in some way enhancing your life in 90 days, move on."

90 Days the New Five Years?

In 2015, I still feel strongly that 90 days is the perfect amount of time, even though the world is moving at a much faster pace than it did when I wrote the above in 2010.

We could say that 90 days is the new five years. If anything, it's giving some projects and people more time than they need or deserve.

Giving something 90 days of my full attention, knowing this is a temporary commitment, allows me to put other top priority projects on hold, on the back burner. After all, it's only for 90 days at the most.

Of course, if you feel great about the experience and results after 90 days, it moves into a degree of permanency in your life. One friend who tried this out, asked his girlfriend to move into his house with him. He had been stalling on this issue, as he was afraid something would go wrong and he might have trouble asking her to leave. But the 90 Day Trial Period gave them a goal to work toward: Making the relationship work for at least 90 days. They agreed to sit down and have contract renewal talks as the 90th day approached. Ten years and counting, they are still together. There were a series of 90 day contract extensions, but after a few of these, both decided they didn't need that strategy any more.

And, in case you were wondering, yes, I did use this strategy when I moved to Panama. One way it manifested itself was that I hardly bought any new possessions that I couldn't fit in the two checked large suitcases and backpack and carry on bag I arrived with. After a lot of tossing and giving away, these were most of my worldly possessions. Two friends are holding some books and papers for me in the U.S., but that's it. There were two exceptions to that rule, however. I had to leave behind my ergonomic computer chair and my desk, so I bought inexpensive versions of each for less than $100 in Panama City. At this writing, I've been living in Panama City for two years and I think the trial period is over. I do notice that I have been making some more major purchases.

Ray Bradbury

One of my favorite mentors and one of only two people I've known that I consider a true genius (the other was Norman Cousins), was Ray Bradbury, who died in 2012 at the age of 92, and was still writing until a few days before his death. I love it when I meet someone who has two qualities that I find irresistible. One is liking what I do in the world, the other is thinking so far out of the box that he or she can create whole new frames of reference or paradigms spontaneously about a lot of different subjects.

In terms of owning your time, Ray told me in one of our many conversations over the years, about his strategy concerning lunch, a simple method of adding a substantial amount of time to his creative day:

"One of the big rules in taking charge of your time is to eliminate lunches with people you don't like. I've gotten rid of lunches from a good part of my life the last fifteen years, which means I've given myself an extra hour-and-a-half every day where I'm not giving my energy away to people who don't appreciate it to start with. People will drain you of your energy and it's gone forever. Stay away from people a certain part of the day and make sure that time belongs to you. If you're not careful, you'll give away your whole life."

Ray's prodigious lifetime creative output is a testimonial to the value of owning your own time. He actually gave me that quote in the early 1980s, when I told him I was thinking about doing a book called **Take Your Time!**

This means he probably saved another twenty years of minutes from lunches he didn't share.

Personally-Styled Timeframes

What matters in any effort, be it business, social, or creative, is not how many hours we put into accomplishing the results we want, but the amount of energy, emotional commitment, and purpose we devote to that effort. In exploring ways of measuring these factors, we can create personally-styled timeframes.

Most people consider time as being well used when they get one of three of my three main criteria in exchange for time:

Knowledge, Pleasure, Profit.

If we start measuring the results of all our time exchanges on the basis of these three things, we can make more intelligent, realistic, and rewarding time choices.

A Time Awareness Exercise

In the past twenty-four hours, can you see clearly the specific amounts of time you exchanged for knowledge, pleasure, or profit?

An example of a simple exchange for knowledge could be attending a lecture or workshop, reading a book or listening to an audio.

An example of exchanging time for pleasure might involve eating at a favorite restaurant with one of your favorite people.

And time you used for profit might be creating or marketing your newest product, service, or idea.

Doing this exercise for a week, or even a month, will give you a sense of whether you have been using most of your time for these three essential objectives in life. It can really get interesting when we combine some or all of these three things in one time exchange. If, for instance, you really love your work, and are learning a lot while doing it, then you've covered all the bases. It's worth taking the time to explore this facet of your life and your time.

Goal Setting

If you thought the above heading meant I was going to tell you how to set goals, and the importance of writing your goals down, forgeddaboutit! I know it drives some of my friends, those who are firmly on Newtonian time, crazy when I say that I think goal-setting can be counter-productive. It often leaves no room for spontaneity, serendipity, and creative mindbursts.

Of course, I have a sense of what my mission in life is, and the creative path I am on, but it's not very specific.

When I emerged from prison, my self-declared intention was to be able to express myself to a much larger audience. I honestly did not know if that would be through doing workshops and focusing on my Moneylove ideas, or writing mystery fiction, or writing and performing a one-man show, or doing stand-up comedy (quite different from a solo theater performance). I also wanted to do something that was worthwhile and important and left a "thumbprint on the world." That great phrase came from psychologist Sid Simon, when he told me for the original **Moneylove** book that it was one of the main reasons people did the work they do.

I did a lot of reflecting, contemplation, meditating on this big decision facing me. After a 12-year absence, how would I reintroduce myself to the world? I left myself open for a totally new creative project or career to show up. I started producing prosperity audio tapes, and took a course at the San Francisco Comedy College, and did stand-up at the famed Purple Onion in San Francisco, as well as a couple of one man performances at the highly respected Marsh Theaters in San Francisco and Berkeley. I even had as an aspiration, becoming the first English language stand-up comedian in Panama.

But as more and more people realized from my blog and audio series, that I was back among the living, it became evident that there was interest in my sticking to the Moneylove track for a while at least. That led to my connecting with my two new Internet and Social Media-savvy partners, and the release of **Moneylove 1.0**, the 1978 book, in digital form, as well as my getting back the rights to my bestselling Nightingale-Conant Moneylove Tapes program and turning that into a digital mp3 format. This book quickly followed. But none of my goals were hard and fast, and I am still leaving myself open to discovering new skills, talents, and options.

Martin Boroson created a statement he has on his wall, and he told me he is not even sure what it means, but he likes it. So do I. It says:

"Everything is optional."

I do believe in goals in the general sense of knowing what I want in my life, but my deadlines are soft ones. If this book isn't ready in a form that is to my satisfaction by early January, 2015, I have no compunction about delaying it, and giving myself time to improve it. (But it was ready!)

The Time Awareness Questions

I believe in the power of asking the right question. I have for many years, and I've used questions a lot in my work. I remember that back in the 1970s, at an Association for Humanistic Psychology conference, a psychiatrist named Dr. Edward Askren (that was his name, really!) did a workshop called, Asking the Right Question. It had such a great impact on me that I did a 100 question questionnaire for my first book, **My Needs, Your Needs, Our Needs**, on relationship communication. It was a list of questions that each person in the relationship asked the other person, going back and forth, though many couples had ways of modifying the process so it worked better for them. It was all about sharing personal experience and knowledge with your partner, with no hard and fast rules, no right or wrong way to use it. A couple of those sample questions:

Name a favorite possession from your past you wished you still had.

Name something you think I hate to do.

Many couples, even those married twenty years or more, said they learned things about their partner they never knew before.

Dr. Wayne Dyer told me my questionnaire was the best exercise he ever used in his classes on marriage counseling. In fact, he looked me up when he moved to South Florida and we spent a fun day together. He was also a great friend when I was in prison, sending me all his books.

At the end of every year, I send close friends a list of over a hundred awareness questions to help them become more aware of what the past year was like and what they would like to have happen in the new year. I've also modified that list to send to coaching clients before our first session, and I ask them to send me back their answers.

So I think you have guessed I am really into using questions for many different purposes. These dozen questions are designed to clarify your personal relationship with time:

1. **Do you often listen to others as to how long some activity should take?**

2. **Are you frequently bored, impatient, or frustrated**

waiting for someone to arrive or something to happen, or while waiting in line?

3. Could you imagine doing your current work in less time than you now devote to it? How much less time?

4. If you had an extra two hours a day, do you know exactly what you'd want to do with them?

5. Did your parents give you any (or many) messages to the effect that there wasn't enough time to do everything that had to be done?

6. How often in any given week do you feel pressured by the clock?

7. When you go to another time zone, do you feel completely out of sorts?

8. Do you have a fixed idea of how long it takes you to get ready for bed?

9. Do you ever take as much or more time planning for an activity than actually doing it?

10. What percentage of your time would you estimate you use to make you a better person?

11. What is the one activity in your life which you consider the most time-wasting? Do you enjoy this activity?

12. On a scale of 1 to 10, 10 being the highest, how much in charge of your time do you feel?

You get to decide for yourself how well you did answering these questions, and what your responses say about you in terms of being a rigid clock-watcher in the tradition of Sir Isaac Newton, or having a much more free view of time and how it operates in your life based on Albert Einstein's model.

I came up with the title, **TimeLove**, because I wanted to make a statement that time was every bit as vital to your personal growth and prosperity and well-being as **Moneylove** was in the area of success and finance.

There was definitely a purpose in all the original **Time Awareness Exercises** I've suggested. It was to give you a greater awareness, a greater knowledge of how you now use time. The application of knowledge is wisdom, so how wise are you going to be about time from now on?

Surplus Time Mentality

I have the view that one of the best and easiest ways to change your life for the better is to develop a Surplus Time Mentality. Now I acknowledge that this is more difficult when you have a family and obligations that take up a good bit of your time, but if you think about how to do it in less time, your subconscious mind will obediently come up with a solution. I have found that this always happens if you have that clear vision of what you want in terms of more time for yourself.

With everyone having exactly 168 hours in each week, what makes the difference are the time attitudes we reinforce by our actions. By using some of the **Time Awareness Exercises**, you can see your own timeframe more clearly. By seeing the extra time you can have in your life, you can begin to think of surplus time as a natural occurrence.

Time and Your Brain

Those parts of your brain involved with intuition, creativity, love, and play are the ones that affect your healthier time perceptions. The Newtonian clock-watching time construct is governed by the rational, logical, methodical part of the brain.

Up to now, the rational part of your brain may have felt comfortable with the fact that seconds, minutes, and hours can be measured--so it all seems to be precise and solid. This is a serious misperception.

We spend a minute looking at a sunset, but we are actually seeing where the sun was eight minutes ago, since that's how long it takes the light to reach us. If we are preoccupied with other thoughts and feelings, that minute might seem much longer than it really is. If you focus all your attention on the sun, thinking of nothing else, with minimal emotional response, it goes by in a flash. What the brain researchers have discovered is that various parts of the brain either speed up or slow down your sense of time. When more of the brain is focused on more detailed and complicated ideas, thoughts, and feelings, it slows down. Single-minded focusing speeds things up. By experimenting with these aspects of our brain, we can truly master time.

Most people see time as spread out with large gaps between thoughts and action. This spread out, horizontal model is slower than the brain processes information. Creative individuals can lose all sense of time when they are engaged in their creative process. In conducting a number of tests in early biofeedback research as a Founding Director of the Biofeedback Institute in New York back in the 1970s, I saw that certain kinds of mental activity were associated with time distortion.

I participated in a number of experiments myself while being connected to brain wave biofeedback equipment for periods of time as long as twelve hours, during which I was mostly in an Alpha or meditative state. Sometimes these sessions seemed to last only ten or fifteen minutes. Again, time was speeding up with a single-minded focusing of the mind.As Martin Boroson said, many people have reported these apparent distortions of time during altered states of consciousness, of which meditation is one of the most natural to achieve.

Time Awareness Exercise

The Blind Feed

One exercise I've facilitated in workshops was so successful, that I want to share it as a Time Awareness Exercise, even though it's a lot more than that. As all good awareness exercises and processes are, it is quite simple. You and a partner prepare some food, and then take turns feeding the partner who is wearing a blindfold. Even though you basically know what food is available, it still comes as a shock to the system when you open your mouth and take in a food item you can't see. First of all, you really have to smell and taste it to figure out what it is. Usually, the exercise is done with the person who is going to be blindfolded filling their own plate, perhaps from a buffet table.

Here's what usually happens. As you focus on other senses, time seems to slow down, so that almost everyone reports thinking the experience was taking a lot longer than the clock indicated. I think this is because, with our eyes closed, we have to pay attention to more things happening at once. They are happening in the same period of time, but it somehow feels fuller and longer. It's also quite usual for individuals to give the signal to stop feeding them when there is much more food left on the plate than they imagined. They were certain they had eaten more. After all, they selected the type of food and how much to put on their plate before being blindfolded, so they are amazed at how much food is left over on the plate.

After trying this out with a good friend or relationship partner, you might try it with a group of people you don't know as well. It's a fantastic exercise for playing with time perception, as well as a great sensual, fun adventure.

Smart Thoughts on Time

Even though Martin Boroson and I are talking about using and expanding and playing with time in a whole new way, it still may be useful to see what other authors have had to say on the subject in the past forty years.

The first I'll mention, was the first book on time management I ever read, Alan Lakein's **How to Get Control of Your Time and Your Life**. Alan became a friend of mine several years after publication of his 1973 bestseller. He's talking more to business people and focused on the Newtonian model, finding ways to get more out of those rigid constructs. One quote he is credited with inventing:

"What is the best use of my time right now?"

Another quote goes well with the concepts in TimeLove:

"Time = Life, Therefore, waste your time and waste your life, or master your time and master your life."

Considering that his book is over forty years old and has sold three million copies, we have to give Alan credit for coming up with some fresh ideas on managing time.

One speaker I met over thirty years ago through the National Speakers Association was Dr. John Lee, who came up with one idea that can really give you a handle on managing your time and making decisions. I don't know if he ever wrote a book on the subject (at least I couldn't find it online), but several of his mentees still talk about "The 4 Ds of Time Management". I talked about it on my Nightingale-Conant Moneylove album (now available in digital form through my blog), and sometimes still use it.

What John came up with was sweet and simple, just the way I like any new process or strategy. He suggested that whenever you have a project, and don't know exactly what to do or where to go with it, apply **The 4 Ds**.

They are to either **Delay it**. **Delegate it**. **Drop it**. Or **Do it.** Could anything be simpler? It prevents a lot of ambiguous thinking about what you want to get done.

Another book, recommended to me by Rupa Cousins, who keeps up with what is happening in the body/mind/spirit world, was written by Stephan Rechtschaffen, M.D. **TIME SHIFTING**: Creating More Time to Enjoy Your Life, was written in 1997. Dr. Rechtschaffen is co-founder of the Omega Institute for Holistic Studies and has taken the path Martin Boroson suggests by moving to Costa Rica for a slower, more mindful way of life. He is director of Blue Spirit in Nosara, Costa Rica. His book is about the relationship between time and stress. I like a statement in the Foreword by spiritual writer, Thomas Moore:

Time is simply one facet of life itself, and life is the gift of time. To wish for time is to wish for life, for the opportunity to live with fullness and vitality. Therefore, time calls for artful attention on our part.

I love that term, "artful attention." In the book itself, Stephan Rechtschaffen writes:

"Do you have enough time in your life? When I ask this question in my seminars on wellness and time, only one or two people generally say yes--out of a class of fifty. When I ask these one or two how they feel, they tend to give a knowing smile: 'I feel great about my life!' is the common answer. Invariably,

these few people say that they consciously changed their relationship with time into one that brings them far more happiness."

Of course this is more confirmation that Martin Boroson and I are on the right path when we suggest you make a conscious effort to change your perceptions and learn to expand, bend, and play with time

Getting away from Newtonian clock time and into more Einsteinian time freedom involves focusing on one thing at a time, learning to slow down and notice our physical and emotional states. It includes getting more in touch with our senses, and what is going on within us and around us in the moment. When we speed up or slow down, noticing what this does to our perception of time is valuable.

So many of us have been conditioned to clock time from an early age-- perhaps when our parents got us our first watch and we kept on hearing, "What time is it?," "What time is it?," as if it was really something important to know.

Time is as important as you want it to be, as you allow it to be. If you give yourself a week to do something, it will certainly not take any less than a week. If you give yourself five years to do something, and I have some friends who are writers working on novels, and they say "It's going to take five years to complete this book." And it will surely take at least five years.

We get a lot of early programming about the importance of time, and the rigidity of time: "Don't be late for school." "Make sure you get up on time." And the things we say about time. "Once upon a time." "Time moves on.""Time is running out." "As time goes by." "Not enough time." Time is very threatening to people who are not leading their own lives, who are not living lives of satisfaction and fulfillment. Slow down the merry-go-round for yourself and start paying attention to how you use time, how you look at time, what you do with time, and realize that you are in charge.

166

Time Awareness Exercise

On a daily basis, look at the amount of time you are completely alone. Get a sense of the quality of that time. Do you feel it's positive or negative time? In other words, is your basic statement, your frame of reference about the alone time in your life "Ahh, it's good to be alone." Or is it closer to, "I can't stand it--I've got to find somebody to be with!" And how creatively do you use your alone time? Do you have a purpose for this time? Take the next week to pay attention to and identify the time you spend alone. Look at how you feel during these times, and see if you can discover a more creative way to use this time.

Sometime during the next week arrange to give yourself on hour of time in which you are completely alone, absolutely alone doing absolutely nothing. And afterwards, write down your feelings and thoughts about this experience. Is your perception of time different when there is no one else around? Does time move faster when you are alone, or slower?

Effective Waiting

Another place you can find some surplus time is when you are waiting. Martin Boroson discusses something we all do concerning time--wait.

Martin:

> *Effective or good waiting is a pre-condition for effective action. If we know how to wait, then we know how to act.*

> *And if you do have a period in which you must wait, because you have no choice but to wait, you can do something incredibly useful in that time to reboot your mind, for example by meditating briefly. There's more value in the waiting if you use that time*

to put yourself in a really good mindset for whatever might be coming.

But in talking about waiting, we really have to consider the incredible pressure that people feel to make decisions quickly, and the pressure we put on our leaders to be "decisive." I think the reason we do that is that we're terrified of anxiety. Waiting, not-knowing, and not having the answer causes anxiety and we hate the anxiety, so we want a so-called decisive leader to make a decision that takes away our anxiety. We have this very strong bias against waiting and against not-knowing.

My belief is that we must learn how to wait better, to sit in the not knowing until the knowing absolutely appears in a very clear way. But because we're so afraid of waiting, we make decisions that haven't been deeply felt or deeply considered, or we make a decision when the time isn't right--just for the sake of making a decision. There will be a time when the action is right, and when the decision appears clearly, but you can't force that. And sometimes that means waiting through a period of great stress and uncertainty.

A useful metaphor for this is a lion at hunt. We think of hunting as an act of dynamic energy and pursuit. And, if you watch a nature documentary, that's what you'll see: the lion pouncing, with dramatic music added in the background (which doesn't exist in nature, of course). But what you don't see, because it doesn't make good television, is that, before pouncing, the lion spent most of its time sitting and waiting for just the right moment. If the lion just pounced willy-nilly, when the chances of a kill were low. Or when it wasn't a good-value kill, that lion would be wasting a tremendous amount of energy.

What the lion has to do is sit and wait for the right moment. But we have a terrible deficit of that ability to wait for the right moment.

Jerry:

I see the same thing in cats, but while one of my cats can sit and wait for an hour or two, he's not going to wait until next Tuesday to act.

Martin:

You know, I probably tend to err on the side of waiting too long to make certain decisions. But a number of times, even when I felt I was waiting too long, something in the universe would happen, new information would appear, and I would think, "Oh my God, I'm so glad I didn't make that decision without having had that piece of information."

My feeling is that if you have a small decision to make, don't wait, just get it over with—be "decisive"—so that you don't stop the flow of life. But if it feels like a big decision, you may want another approach, a more wisdom-based approach to decision-making that may require some patience. By this I mean looking for, waiting for, the big vision, which might involve going on retreat, contemplating, brainstorming, dreaming. In a wisdom-based decision-making process we ask the deeper questions: What's the real goal here? What's the real purpose of my life? What is the real opportunity? We look for insight from a deeper source within ourselves.

I don't claim to have the only answer on this. I can certainly see the advantage of being "decisive" sometimes, and I believe that even after a decision is made, you can adapt. Sometimes I think you should just leap before you look, and other times you don't want to act prematurely just to have made a decision. And sometimes the impulse to make an immediate decision comes from fear, not from wisdom. And then there are certain people who deliberate too long about decisions, because they're afraid they're going to get it wrong. It's a really hard thing to know the right way to do it, but I just want to make the case for the value of waiting and looking within.

Jerry:

Yes, and I think you have to trust your gut, your inner knowing. Is it time to make a fast decision, or will I gain more wisdom and make a better decision if I wait awhile.

Martin:

The skill is in getting to know when the time is right. And if you're good at knowing when the time is right, there's no anxiety in waiting. Wisdom is in knowing when the time is right.

Ken Keyes, Jr.

One aspect of this, I thought of after my conversation with Martin Boroson, was originally inspired by another friend and mentor, the late Ken Keyes, Jr., author of the multimillion copy bestseller, **The Handbook to Higher Consciousness.** He came up with a list of what he called 12 Pathways to Higher Consciousness, and one of the ones that impressed me most was:

I act freely when I am tuned in, centered, and loving, but, if possible, I avoid acting when I am emotionally upset and depriving myself of the wisdom that flows from love and expanded consciousness.

Ever since I came across Ken Keyes' *12 Pathways* in the 1970s, I have used this one as a model, a guide. So, the first thing I do when I am about to make a major life-changing decision is ask myself, "Am I emotionally upset as I think about making this decision?" If I am angry or sad, I delay the decision.

If you look back on your own life, you may well find that many of those decisions you made quickly in a moment of emotional upset or turmoil didn't turn out very well.

Here's a story (or parable) about the frustration and anxiety caused by waiting:

The Race Horse

A friend just emailed me from England to tell me he was heading for the races at Ascot. This conjured up all sorts of images of elegant people milling about, especially beautiful women in beautiful hats, as recalled from that famous scene in My Fair Lady.

But then I got to thinking about the poor main attraction, the race horse, champing at the bit in the stable stall, waiting for his moment of glory as thousands of people were more involved in eating strawberries and cream than in caring about him. And then, finally, he is led up to the track itself, put into the starting gate, and still he has to wait. What for? Before he is even allowed to participate he has to wait for the starter to open up the gate and let him go.

He is in a cramped, frustrating prison, until someone yells, "They're off!" and he is free to show his stuff. And if something goes wrong, and the gate has a mechanical failure and doesn't open, or opens a second or two late, he is finished before he starts.

Think about your own situation. Are you waiting for someone to open the gate for you? Are you frustrated and champing at the bit, ready to run the race, to show what you can do, but you just can't seem to get started?

What separates us human beings from race horses, magnificent creatures that they are, is that we can open our own starting gate. So what are you waiting for?

Editor's Notes:

We hope you've enjoyed Volume One of Moneylove 3.0 and that you've gotten great results from the various exercises listed within. Please join us in Volume Two which includes the next 4 Books of Moneylove 3.0. In this volume, Jerry covers additional fascinating topics and offers more of his unique and highly effective exercises. Here is a quick preview:

Book Six: Carpe Serendipity -Whether you call them coincidences, happy accidents, or Godwinks, this book is about your opening up time and space to have more of them occur, and how to optimize them when they arrive.

Book Seven: Building a Prosperous Spirit -Becoming more prosperous has always been a spiritual quest, and many of the best prosperity teachers have come from that world. Here, some of the wisest join Jerry in guiding the way to a more prosperous spirit, and connecting the metaphysical world of visions and dreams with the physical reality of material success.

Book Eight: Cyber Consciousness -With the help of some of the most successful young Internet entrepreneurs in the world, we explore the power and potential of online prosperity, along with the pitfalls to avoid.

Book Nine: Jobs and No Jobs -The first part of this book explores entrepreneurial lessons from Steve Jobs, while the second part gives new insights into why being self-employed may be the surest route to prosperity.

Additional Resources:

We are very pleased to continue Jerry's policy of always giving people more than their money's worth, as such we've got two great offers for you.

First, by visiting the link below, you will receive two free bonus audios which contain more of Jerry's innovative ideas and concepts.

www.p4nm.com/freemoneyloveaudios

Also...

We are very happy to provide an exclusive Free Offer related to the Go-Mode Success Tracker Program mentioned several times in Moneylove 3.0.

3.0. Please visit the link below to receive a FREE Copy of the book, "Go-Mode the End of Mediocrity" as well as a very special offer on the Go-Mode Success Tracker.

www.gomodetracker.com/moneylovefre eoffer

*The Go-Mode Success Tracker is the fun and easy to use accountability tool that is described by many as the most effective personal development resource on the market today.

And the Lord,
Your guard
will make you
abundantly
prosperous in
all your undertakings
Deuteronomy
30:9